Shadow Over America

JOHN D. FREEMAN

Convention Press

NASHVILLE   TENNESSEE

Printed in the United States of America
160. JUL 56 R.R.D.

About the Author

THE AUTHOR was born on a farm near Allene, Arkansas, the son of John D. and Mecha Wright Freeman. He received his A.B. degree from the University of Arkansas, the M.A. from Duke University, and the Th.M. from the Southern Baptist Theological Seminary. Ouachita College of Arkansas, Union University of Tennessee, and Georgetown College of Kentucky have given him the D.D. degree. In recognition of his contribution to the field of rural life, the University of Arkansas gave him in 1950 the degree of Doctor of Humane Letters.

He married Landis Barton of Dallas, Texas, in 1918. They have two children, Mrs. C. Franklin Fielden, Jr., of Colorado Springs, Colorado, and Mrs. Perry M. White, Jr., of Spearman, Texas. He served as pastor of West Broadway Baptist Church, Louisville, Kentucky; First Baptist, Springfield, Kentucky; and Belmont Heights Baptist, Nashville, Tennessee. From 1925 to 1933 he was editor of *The Baptist and Reflector,* Tennessee; 1933-42, executive secretary, Tennessee Baptist Convention; 1942-46, editor, *The Western Recorder,* Kentucky; 1946-50, field secretary, Rural Department, Baptist Home Mission Board. Author of *More Than Money, Time's Character Gauge, Rural Church, Death Loses the Game,* etc. Residence, 1806 Ashwood Avenue, Nashville 12, Tennessee.

Foreword

"THE LOVE of money is the root of all evil" (1 Tim. 6: 10). It is the love of money that impels people to engage in questionable practices and to promote business enterprises which are in no sense necessary for human well-being. The love of money leads otherwise good people to override conscience and common sense in order to engage in such practices as gambling, using short weights and measures, various forms of thievery, the operation of houses of ill-fame, and all methods of dispensing alcoholic beverages—liquor store, dispensary, tavern, cabaret, night club, roadhouse, and bootlegging joint.

The manufacture and sale of alcoholic beverages comes under the class of business enterprises which produce profits by degrading customers. For ages this fact has been recognized by various leaders, many of whom have sought to curb the business or to destroy it altogether. Numerous exposures of the nature of alcohol have been made and of its effects upon the human body. Chief among the investigators have been members of medical societies and heads of welfare agencies. Some two centuries ago Christian churches joined the effort to expose and outlaw alcohol. That struggle, which over a period of centuries has grown powerful and then lost force, is again getting under way in America and other nations.

In the limited space provided in this volume it is impossible to do more than give a few facts and to offer some pertinent suggestions. To learn just how large is the store of information on the subject one needs only to visit the alcohol and drug section of any large library. Many volumes have been written and statistics have been compiled from thousands of sources to show how alcohol harms the body, unseats the nerve controls, and unleashes the baser nature of its victims; how it breaks up homes, corrupts government, increases crime, and adds to society's tax load. It is the hope of the author that the information given herein and the suggestions presented may arouse such interest that further study of the subject may be made. It is his ardent wish that an increasing number of informed workers may go into the field to battle against the forces which, for the sake of easy gain, are ever ready to promote the trade in alcoholic beverages, to entice every possible person to patronize their business, and thereby, whether wittingly or not, to hasten the overthrow of the democracy which we proudly call America.

JOHN D. FREEMAN

Nashville, Tennessee

Contents

I. NATURE'S ALCHEMY
   1. The Heart of Wine
   2. Divinely Established Control

II. FERMENTATION AND FOOD
   1. An Odd Plant
   2. A Cruel Worm
   3. A Deep Secret
   4. Control or Ruin

III. THE DIVINE PURPOSE
   1. An Ordained Place
   2. Society's Obligation
   3. Mythology Bears Witness

1

A POTENT PRODUCT

"AND that's the story, Clerk, just as it happened. From being a reputable citizen, with a comfortable home, a good business, and a lovely young wife, I am now a vagabond, working here and there only to secure money with which to try to quench a thirst that grows more terrible with every drink I buy."

The speaker paused for a moment, with the look of a haunted creature in his eyes; then he banged the counter before him with clenched hand and cried, "Why do men do it, Clerk? Why?"

It was August, 1912, in a construction camp near Van Buren, Arkansas. The author was in charge of the commissary and boarding cars of a crew that was laying heavy steel rails on the Frisco Railway. Bill Day, one of the "gang," had come into the commissary car one rainy afternoon and, finding the author alone, had unburdened his troubled soul.

Bill told of his enviable state a few months before in a suburban area of Kansas City. He had owned a retail grocery and the two-story building which housed it. He and a bride of a few months lived in the upper story. But instead of cultivating Christian friendships, they spent their Sundays in a near-by club where dancing and petty gambling furnished the chief attractions and where alcoholic beverages broke down inhibitions and

1

self-control and led to license in conduct. This went on for several months during which he and his wife drank more freely and gradually developed a craving for alcoholic drinks. Then the pleasure-seeking paid off in a terrible way: Bill returned to the apartment one Saturday night and found a note on the dresser in their bedroom. It read:

"Bill, I'm tired of the store and of your being in it so much of the time. When you get this I will be on my way with Charlie to another city; do not try to follow me."

"At first I could not believe my eyes," Bill concluded. "So I went to the club and there learned the truth. Then I got on a bender and, when I sobered up weeks later, I had nothing left of my business and property. My reputation was gone and I discovered that I was a slave to this awful thirst. My wife had secured a divorce; my world had tumbled down about my head." And he ended the story with the frantic question, "Why?" which countless victims of the thirst for alcohol have voiced.

From the confession which Bill Day made that day and the question which he uttered with such vehemence, the author, for the first time, began to realize just how potent is the product of fermentation and how very dangerous it is when not controlled.

I. NATURE'S ALCHEMY

For one to understand beverage alcohol he must know its nature and its effects upon the human body. He can gain this knowledge from many authentic sources. Medical science, sociology, history, and penology give it. This chapter will show by the explanation of scientific facts just what alcohol is and give some reasons why it should be controlled.

1. *The Heart of Wine*

There are in our world some three-quarters of a million things which are called substance. Of this vast number, about six hundred thousand contain carbon in one form or another. Alcohol, in whatever form it may appear, contains this product which is in reality stored sunshine, or solar energy. Wine, beer, gin, and all other intoxicating beverages contain ethyl alcohol which is composed of two parts of carbon, six parts of hydrogen and one of oxygen, the symbol being C_2H_5OH. Water, nature's perfect beverage, contains two parts of hydrogen and one of oxygen, H_2O.

Just why does adding two parts of carbon and four more parts of hydrogen convert water into alcohol? No one can answer that question. When the tiny plant known as yeast excretes an enzyme called zymase and it takes hold of the substance called sugar, the result is alcohol which is the heart of wine and all intoxicants.

2. *Divinely Established Control*

Alcohol was designed by the Creator to meet certain needs in the chemical world and to serve mankind in many helpful ways. It was never intended to be used as a beverage. As is true with all of the products of nature's great laboratory, alcohol must be held in its ordained place and to its predetermined tasks else it becomes dangerous, as can be proved anywhere by the simple experiment of sprinkling a tender plant with alcohol instead of water. God never intended high explosives to be made into playthings for children, yet every year, because society does not maintain rigid control of the manufacture and sale of fireworks, little folks are maimed or killed by them. Likewise, he did not intend that people should misuse the narcotic in alcoholic beverages.

One reads a great deal about wine drinking in France, Italy, and elsewhere in Europe, usually seeing in any report some reference to the lack of drunkenness in such areas. What he does not read is that the native or low-grade wines, drunk so freely by the peasants, seldom contain more than 5 per cent of alcohol, hence do not produce drunkenness as readily as do the liquors that contain from two to five times the alcoholic content of such wines. Nature set the limit of alcohol which fermentation produces at 14 per cent, but she, at the same time, set the limit upon the amount of alcohol which one can drink with impunity at zero! Scientific tests prove that drinking a small quantity of alcohol causes almost immediate disturbances in the brain of one who imbibes.

II. FERMENTATION AND FOOD

1. *An Odd Plant*

Alcohol comes as a result of chemical action which is produced by a microscopic plant, the most familiar form of which is found in yeast. It consists of minute egg-shaped cells which multiply by budding. Under temperatures from 70° to 100° Fahrenheit, and when put in any moist substance containing sugar, they multiply with great rapidity. They may be kept for long periods in a dry cake in temperatures under 100°. Sub-zero temperature does not kill them.

When this tiny plant is put at a friendly temperature into any substance containing sugar, it begins to feed upon the saccharine content. The yeast cells, so small that thirty thousand of the smallest ones would reach only one inch if placed side by side, feed upon the sweets. In turn they excrete, expel as offal from their bodies, an enzyme, a mysterious and complicated substance which can produce chemical action without being absorbed or destroyed in the process. This enzyme is called "zymase" and it changes the sugar into carbon dioxide and alcohol.

It is as if one were standing beside a machine in which tiny workers were touching with magic wands the particles of one substance and causing them to disappear while in their places appear two other substances. One of these moves the mixture in the vat, causing it to bubble and foam. This is the carbon dioxide gas, lighter than air, hence rising in the vat. The other is the alcohol which remains in the vat. The zymase goes on with its work and accumulates in mass while the yeast cells have food upon which to act. One could never have grasped the full meaning of the words of Paul, "A little leaven leaveneth the whole lump" (1 Cor. 5:6), had this secret of the process of fermentation not been discovered. A tiny bit of yeast, put into a bushel of flour when the flour is moistened, soon produces a vast amount of zymase which in turn carries on the fermentation.

2. A Cruel Worm

Alcohol evaporates at 173° Fahrenheit, hence can readily be separated from any liquid containing it. Water boils at 212° at sea level. So, before it is hot enough for much of it to be evaporated, the alcohol has boiled and passed from the mixture. In order to condense the alcohol it is forced through a coiled pipe which is kept cool. Because copper resists the chemical action of alcohol better than other available metals, it is used in the distillation process. The pipe, so familiar in areas where moonshining is carried on, is called the "worm." To keep it cool so as to make condensation more efficient, the moonshiner immerses it in a barrel through which water continuously flows. But what a difference between the water and that which comes out of the worm!

Whether used by the licensed distiller or by the back-woods moonshiner, this worm turns out the same product. The small copper pipe of the moonshiner, coiled inside a barrel through which water from a creek flows, is crude indeed when compared with the ornate and expensive equipment of the big distillery, but the liquid that drips from its end into a jug contains the same narcotic drug that flows into the barrel in the big factory. Whether sold as "bottled in bond" or as "corn likker," the distiller's worm produces a dangerous habit-forming, character-undermining liquid, and history proves that whosoever is deceived thereby is not wise.

3. A Deep Secret

Every living thing must have water. Man has used it for ages with never a thought about what it is and why. Skilled men at last learned that it is made up of two invisible gases. Further research proved that these two sources of energy are related as follows: two parts of hydrogen to one part of oxygen. The mystery of the chemical compound lies in a twofold field: just what is each of these elements and why are they, when separate, invisible? Why is it, when they are united in the ratio of two to one, that they produce a visible substance which is called water? Let him answer who can.

During high school days many a student learns these facts about water. The author spent many pleasant hours in a laboratory, separating the two elements with electric wires, catching each in a separate test tube, and experimenting with them. Today's student has a far more thrilling experience in learning of the two invisible energies that make the atom which, half a century ago, was considered the ultimate, indestructible unit of the material world. But, whether dealing with the separate elements or with the atoms which make each, one always sees the same—proof of the operation of inviolable, unchangeable laws in the chemical world.

Another part of the mystery is found in the fact that when the two elements which compose water are separated and then brought together again under the right conditions, the result is the production of intense heat. Before electric welding came along and before the fission of the atom brought usable atomic energy, the hottest flame man knew was produced by the oxyhydrogen blowpipe. Yet the energies that made it possible are the same that give the world water! There is little wonder that the wise men who prepared the King James Version of the Bible did not render 2 Peter 3:7 in keeping with one significant meaning of the Greek text, "The heavens and the earth which are now stored with fire" (ASV marg.). Only an omniscient, omnipotent Creator could have foreseen man's numerous, universal needs for fire and water or have provided them through the two elements and stored the planet on which he lives with an inexhaustible supply of each.

But this same beneficent Creator also made man

capable of possessing enough wisdom and knowledge to use these and all other substances in the right manner. One cannot find on history's pages the record of any people, however primitive they may have been, who tolerated the uncontrolled use of either fire or water. Social control has prevailed even among the Hottentots! To argue, therefore, that the social control of the manufacture and distribution of alcoholic beverages, or of any other dangerous substance, is contrary to good judgment makes one flaunt his prejudices in the face of the universal opinion of the human family as well as the direct revelation of God.

4. *Control or Ruin*

Between Cleveland, Tennessee, and Murphy, North Carolina, one passes through a large mountainous section where the vegetation has been destroyed, with the result that devastating erosion has cut grinning gullies down the hillsides and turned a once lovely mountain section into a striking picture of utter desolation. Copper Hill, Ducktown, and smaller towns are situated in this area, marking locations of mine entrances and of smelters.

When the smelting industry got under way decades ago, crude methods of disposing of the refuse were employed. A by-product of the smelting was sulphuric acid, a deadly enemy of vegetation. The fumes bearing this poison spread over the countryside, the gas settled down about the plants, and before many years had passed all vegetation in the section was destroyed. After the region had been ravished, and silt from the eroding hills had completely filled the lake above a near-by power dam, owners of the properties began to give serious attention to what had happened. Then, aided by soil conservation forces of the state and the nation, they set to work to reclaim the waste places.

Their first problem was to dispose of the deadly fumes from the smelters. Soon these were being stripped of their sulphuric acid content and this heavy, powerful chemical was being turned to useful tasks. Now sulphuric acid is one of the very profitable by-products of the copper smelters, and millions of tons of it are used annually in our land in the production of paper, plastics, and other products made from plant fibers. So, that which destroys plant life when uncontrolled, transforms, when controlled, the fibers of such plants into miracle products for the benefit of man.

Just as unrestrained gases wrought havoc in the East Tennessee mountains, so does any other product do harm when not used as the Creator intended. Alcohol is no exception. On every hand one sees the wreckage which it produces when it is placed by license in the hands of people, the sole purpose of one group being to gain easy profits and of another to use it to stir up the natural body processes and secure what is for the moment a pleasing sensation. What a scene of devastation one lays bare when he presents excerpts from the reports of the Federal Bureau of Investigation, of traffic officers throughout the nation, and revelations which any welfare agency can furnish. See the havoc in America!

Over four and one half million chronic alcoholics whose distressing condition represents a potential loss of eight billion man hours which at the new minimum wage scale of one dollar per hour equals eight billion dollars! Annually more than 37,000 people are killed because of traffic accidents upon our highways and streets. Of these, conservative estimates put the number slaughtered because of drinking drivers, or because of pedestrians made careless by strong drink, at 25 per cent, or a total of 9,250. The total sum spent by American people for alcoholic beverages is above ten billion dollars per year! The total crime bill mounts higher and higher, running over fifteen billion dollars a year! Facilities in veterans' hospitals are overcrowded everywhere and an appalling proportion of the former servicemen demanding this hospitalization are victims of alcoholic beverages. There are many slum areas where poverty and crime abound in spite of the unprecedented prosperity that has blessed the nation for several years. At least a million people in the nation now suffer some degree of permanent, crippling injury because of accidents on streets and highways, accidents most of which never would have occurred had it not been for uncontrolled alcohol.

The picture cannot be presented in a few words. One must read the daily newspapers, visit emergency wards of the hospitals, and consult police officers and highway patrolmen; he must visit homes where hungry women and ragged children await with fearful hearts the homecoming of an alcoholic husband and father; he must sit in divorce courts, beside juvenile judges, and on juries in criminal courts. Why the awful picture? Because society does not have wisdom enough to control the manufacture and use of this compound.

One feature of a television news roundup was a scene beside the great freeway in Los Angeles, California, along which the heaviest traffic of the world speeds. The reporter was talking with a traffic officer; a motorcycle officer stopped a car on the freeway. Then the driver was given various tests which clearly revealed that he was partially intoxicated. "How much is too much drinking for a driver?" the reporter finally asked, and the traffic chief replied, "One drink is too much." It can be declared emphatically that, to prevent the taking of that one drink, society is compelled to control both the manufacture and the distribution of alcohol, whatever be the form in which it may appear.

III. The Divine Purpose

1. *An Ordained Place*

There is a place for alcohol, else it would not be here. It will be a boon or a bane according as man uses it. If it is used as God intended it to be, it brings good; if, on the other hand, man prostitutes its use for the gratification of his lust for temporal pleasure or for gain, it brings a definite curse.

The artist makes alcohol his tool in the production and blending of colors that go into a lovely painting. The wise mechanic makes it generate power by means of which he can produce things that help his fellows. The chemist makes it his tool in the production of varnishes, paints, insecticides, germicides, and other beneficial products. The pharmacist uses it to bring into solution or to preserve various chemicals without which human illnesses would be more difficult to control. Were this strange liquid used only in keeping with the divine purpose, there would be no occasion for the endless struggle to destroy the traffic in alcoholic beverages, which is so profitable that people will carry it on even when they know how it blasts and ruins the customers whom they serve.

2. Society's Obligation

How alcohol is used is as much the business of society as is the use of sulphuric acid or atomic energy. Society is under as much obligation to control its manufacture and sale as it is to control the use of highways, or the manufacture and distribution of explosives, or the use of all forms of opiates. It is as much the business of good citizens to control alcoholic beverages as it is for the farmer to keep the weeds from damaging or destroying his crops, or the termites from eating down his house.

It is true that there is no sin in alcohol; the sin is in the hearts of human beings. In hands that are not restrained by wisdom and brotherly love or by society's control, alcohol becomes dangerous. More than one person has learned that it bites like a serpent and stings like an adder (Prov. 23:32). As it was in the days of Solomon and long before, "Wine is a mocker" (Prov. 20:1) and strong drink continues to be drunk by foolish people. They who are wise will refuse to be deceived by the astute and richly endowed advertising campaigns of people who gain big profits by making and selling the beverages which contain this subtle and powerful narcotic.

3. Mythology Bears Witness

Records of the beliefs about origins, and theories about various mysteries which life thrusts before people hold for the student valuable information. The myths which any race accumulated during its primitive days bring to the student facts which enable him to know about the past as well as about the people whose traditions have thus been preserved. So, much about primitive man's attitude toward alcohol may be learned from mythology.

In writing his sacred book, the Koran, Mohammed included some rather severe rules against the use of intoxicants. It is believed by some scholars that he was influenced in his attitude toward intoxicants by a story which he must have learned when a lad. That myth states that on one occasion the Almighty sent two angels to govern the earth and to act as arbitrators when men had difficulties that threatened to end in strife. Having learned of their ministry, a beautiful woman invited them to her home where great trouble threatened to separate her and her husband.

At the meal which she served the guests, wine was offered and the angels were so enticed by the beauty of the hostess that they forgot the restrictions which governed them and drank of it. As often happens when politeness impels one to drink an alcoholic beverage which the host or hostess has set before him, the messengers took too much and became intoxicated. Then improper advances were made to the lovely hostess who in turn secured the keys to heaven from one of them and went to present her cause to the Almighty. Allah heard her report and condemned the two angels to be hung by their heels over the abyss to await the coming judgment. Then the Almighty put a ban on the use of wine by mankind.

SUGGESTED TOPICS FOR DISCUSSION

1. Relate incidents you know about in which alcohol played a deadly role in destroying life, property, or reputation.
2. Make a list of various products which, like alcohol, prove harmful to man if misused. Classify these as "controlled" and "uncontrolled."
3. What useful products require alcohol in their preparation or preservation?

CHAPTER 2 OUTLINE

2

SHADOWS OVER THE PAST

THE Macedonian king who reigned for thirteen years (336–323 B.C.) is often used as an illustration of the tragedy of unrestrained lust. "Alexander the Great conquered the world before he was forty and died prematurely because he could not conquer himself" is the familiar quotation.

Alexander's father, Philip II, had made great headway toward establishing a union of all Hellenic peoples but fell a victim of the jealous rage of Alexander's mother who had been put away for another wife. Outraged by this betrayal, perhaps like Jacob's mother wanting to promote the interests of her son, she had Philip assassinated in 336 B.C. So, in his twentieth year Alexander took over the task of ruling and within ten years had won the title "Alexander the Great."

This brilliant youth who inspired Napoleon and Adolph Hitler had been taught by Aristotle and trained in war by his renowned father. Taking over the reins of government he soon conquered the rebellious provinces to the south and forced the senate of Corinth to make him commander of the Panhellenic armies. He then overran Asia Minor. In 331 he met and defeated Darius and captured Persepolis, the capital of Persia, where he took vast stores of booty which helped to enlarge and strengthen his armies. At last great Babylon fell before his forces and then followed the celebration which ended in death.

The palace of the defeated king was the scene of riotous and prolonged feasting. One evening Alexander, already far gone in his cups, drained the Cup of Hercules, a great tankard that held six bottles of wine. Altogether intoxicated by that time, he set forth to prove that he was more powerful than Hercules, so tried to empty the cup again, with the result that he became violently ill and died a few days later, at the age of thirty-three. Of his going the famous philosopher, Seneca, wrote: "Here then is this hero, invincible by all the toils of prodigious marches, by dangers of sieges and combats, by the most violent extremes of heat and cold, here he lies conquered by intemperance and struck to earth by the fateful Cup of Hercules."

I. ANCIENT RECORDS AND ALCOHOL

As long as man has set down records of his deeds there have been reports of the use of fermented liquors and their effects upon individuals as well as upon society. Pictures in Egyptian tombs, among the ruins of Pompeii and elsewhere, show both drinking and revelries and the sorry state to which drinking often leads the victims.

1. *A Red Light from the Past*

Egyptians do not seem to have had wines, except those imported for sacramental purposes, until the seventh century before Christ. The Hebrews very probably introduced the use of wines but not grape culture. The imported wine was more expensive than the native malt beverages which continued to be the chief alcoholic drink. One ancient record praises an Egyptian mother whose daily care of her son included portions of loaves and beer. Although she lived twenty-seven hundred years before Christ, she has her imitators today! Two thousand years later Herodotus, the historian, found the Egyptians still using beer. Plutarch indicates that the importation of wine by Egyptians did not reach large proportions prior to 600 B.C.

Plutarch also says that strict prohibition laws were in force prior to that date. Priests in their rituals were limited to small portions of wine, while they who served at the altars of Osiris and Isis were forbidden any. Knowledge of the harmful effects of wine upon their rulers is shown by the law which limited very strictly the portion of wine which the ruler could drink. Thus it is seen that statutory regulation of strong drink began centuries before the Christian era.

An Egyptian military officer who lived about the time of Moses declared, "If beer gets into a man, it overcomes his mind . . . thou knowest that wine is an abomination." Josephus reports that during an Egyptian feast which the king attended, "The butler pressed the grapes into a goblet. Having strained the sweet wine, he gave it to the king to drink." The Greek word for such wine was *gluekos* (glucose).

Rameses II ruled Egypt from 1324 to 1288 B.C. It was during his reign that Moses came upon the scene. From Josephus as well as from the Bible much can be learned about this foundling prince. Reared in the palace means he was given the best education the royal family could command. He was familiar from youth with the customs of the royal family, with their feasts and other celebrations, and with the religious beliefs and ritual. He can, therefore, be relied upon when his record is studied.

In the great psalm which Moses delivered to the elders
of the Hebrews just before his death (Deut. 32), he
castigated them for their backslidings, their disregard
of the commandments of God, and their tendency to
turn to pagan gods. That he well knew the evils of alcoholic beverages is attested by his description of the
vintages which Israel's enemies provided: "Their vine
is of the vine of Sodom, and of the fields of Gomorrah:
their grapes are grapes of gall, their clusters are bitter"
(Deut. 32:32 asv).

Ancient records also tell of the perfidy of Noah (Gen.
9:20–21). As is usually the case where alcohol is concerned, others besides the drinker must suffer. While
Ham must have committed a far worse crime than merely
to look at his father's naked body, the fact remains that
had the father not been drunk the son would not have had
opportunity to sin as he did. Likewise the incest between
Lot and his daughters was due to strong drink (Gen. 19:
31–38).

"Woe unto them that rise up early in the morning,
that they may follow strong drink; that continue until
night, till wine inflame them! And the harp, and the viol,
the tabret, and pipe, and wine, are in their feasts: but
they regard not the work of the Lord, neither consider
the operation of his hands. . . . Woe unto them that are
mighty to drink wine, and men of strength to mingle
strong drink." These words from Isaiah (5:11–12, 22)
describe scenes in modern night clubs, roadhouses, and
mixing bars.

2. Ancient Religions Fought Alcohol

People should not be misled by the propaganda which
places opposition to legalized alcoholic beverages at the

hands of a few fanatical Christians. Ages ago pagan religions opposed wine and beer and stronger drinks. The Rig Veda, sacred book of the Hindus, tells much about the use of wine in the Buddhist ceremonies. It pictures the gods as excessive drinkers and approves of the libations which were freely offered to the gods, the priests, of course, drinking much of the wines which worshipers brought as offerings.

But all of the people were not beguiled by the wine or misled by the priests. There were wise men in India who fought the drunkenness, and finally a ruler arose who sought to put an end to so much of it. The Sacred Laws of Manu, written about 500 B.C., prohibited the manufacture of three alcoholic drinks. These statutes set penalties for drunkenness. The lay offender was branded on the forehead and ostracized from social groups. The priest who became drunk was condemned to be reborn as an insect or a fierce beast. Prohibition, as before indicated, was strictly enforced in Egypt and the laws had their origin in the religion of the day.

3. Examples of Tragedy

Cyrus the Great of Persia once destroyed an enemy force by pretending to retreat from the battlefield so hurriedly that he had to abandon large supplies of food and wine. The enemy fell into his trap, gorged themselves, and became drunk. Then Cyrus returned and overwhelmed them. Centuries later, however, the wine cup had so debauched the Persians that the Saracens, whose religious founder, Mohammed, included in their sacred book, the Koran, a prohibition against the use of intoxicants, readily conquered them.

William Hogarth (1697–1764) gave the world two

masterpieces of art, paintings in which is depicted the sorry state to which the uncontrolled traffic in alcoholic beverages leads man. One of these is *Beer Street.* It shows a tavern beside a street in an English town. Holding the center of the scene is a fat, well-dressed man, a long-stemmed pipe in his hand, a tanker of ale on a table beside him, and a voluptuous woman on his lap, with one arm about his neck. Other revelers are scattered about, some of them on the roof of a near-by residence, indicating their utter disregard for the rights of other people. *Gin Lane* shows the victims of strong drink as they pawn furniture, clothes, and other articles to get money with which to buy more drinks. In the foreground is a ragged child gnawing a bone which a mangy dog is ready to grab. A mother is pouring some ale down the throat of an infant. Through a window in the background can be seen the finished product of *Gin Lane,* a suicide hanging in full view of the street. Hogarth presented in these two paintings scenes that all who have ever worked in a "skid row" section know. Such welfare workers also recognize that denizens of skid rows are reduced to squalor and degeneracy by alcoholic beverages which society permits some of her members to place at the disposal of the citizenry.

II. ABSTINENCE PAYS

For ages man has been familiar with the evil effect of alcoholic beverages upon human flesh. From many records one may find stories of famous athletes, as well as leaders in business, politics, and in society in general in which the benefits which are enjoyed by people who refused to use alcoholic beverages are set forth or in which lives of them who used it have been ruined.

1. Ancient Hebrews Warned

An ancient king named Lemuel tells of advice which his mother had given him. No advocate of abstinence today could set truth more succinctly: "Give not thy strength unto women, nor thy ways to that which destroyeth kings. It is not for kings, O Lemuel, it is not for kings to drink wine; nor for princes strong drink: lest they drink, and forget the law, and pervert the judgment of any of the afflicted" (Prov. 31:3–5). Another well-known moralist stated the same truth in these words: "Whoredom and wine and new wine take away the heart" (Hos. 4:11). The sage, who wrote under the pseudonym "The Preacher," tells how he sought to cheer his flesh with wine, to secure an education, and to check the paths of folly, in order to discover what "was good for the sons of man"; but in the end he discovered how terribly he had been deceived by this "vanity and striving after the wind" (Eccl. 2:3, 11 marg.). Throughout the Old Testament, one finds God's condemnation of indulgence in strong drink and against them who make it available to the people.

2. Hebrew Youths Defiant

The Hebrew youths who had been captured by Nebuchadnezzar and taken to Babylon (625 b.c.) have been used innumerable times to encourage young people to abstain both from alcoholic beverages and from rich foods. Whoever trained those lads had the same opinion of drinking and gormandizing that a modern football coach has. To achieve superiority in athletics the athlete must abstain from alcoholic drinks.

At the time Daniel and his three friends were carried

captive (Daniel 1), Babylon was a great land, but the seeds of degeneracy were already springing up, especially in the capital city. The priests of the pagan gods exacted a heavy toll from the people in food and wine. By precept as well as by example these religious leaders led their followers, including the rulers, into excesses, praising the virtues of wine and assuring the public that it was the will of the gods for them to drink it freely. Daniel, Shadrach, Meshach, and Abednego had their home in the palace grounds and were supposed to conform to the pattern of life that prevailed. But, unlike aspirants for social prestige in this day, they refused to follow the customs, and put in jeopardy their partial freedom rather than yield to a form of slavery which they knew to be the lot of them who drink. So they begged for and were granted the right to eat simple food and to drink no wine for a testing period; the result was a victory for youth and for abstinence. No one need be afraid of the outcome of such a test.

3. *Nazirites Abstained*

When God wanted a big man for an important task, he never chose an alcoholic woman to be the mother, and he required that the son be a total abstainer. The Bible tells of three noted Nazirites—Samson, Samuel, and John the Baptist. We learn about Samson's consecration from Judges 13:7, 16–17; of Samuel's from 1 Samuel 1; and of John the Baptist's from Luke 1. The records give us three significant facts: the mother who would give a dedicated son must abstain from alcoholic beverages; the son who would develop into a leader was never to touch intoxicants in any form; the youth was to be subjected to a rigid regimen with no rich foods and no other form of self-indulgence. Unshorn hair, unshaven beard, rough plain clothes, and restricted social life marked such young men. Samson lost his power when he allowed Delilah to wheedle from him the secret of his strength. One wonders if she first had not led him to drink wine.

4. How About Timothy?

No Bible character has been used with more zest by friends of legalized liquor than Timothy. The author once heard a voluble, vociferous man haranguing a crowd beside a street in Fayetteville, Arkansas. Impelled by curiosity, he joined the crowd and soon learned that the speaker was preaching a sermon for the liquor interests and that his text was, "Drink no longer water, but use a little wine for thy stomach's sake and thine often infirmities" (1 Tim. 5:23). Williams very accurately translates this, "Stop drinking water only, but take a little wine to strengthen your stomach and relieve its frequent attacks." The street preacher did not quote any of the biblical denunciations of strong drink.

What is the truth about Timothy? Paul wrote to one afflicted with some form of dysentery. He very probably was passing on instructions from Luke the physician. Nowhere does Paul advocate the use of wine as a beverage. Many gastro-intestinal ailments of Paul's day were due to contaminated water, even as they are in many countries today. Paul took care to limit the dosage of this remedy—"a little wine." The alcohol in wine acted as a germicide to destroy the vicious germ and thus was a proved remedy. To use this passage in defense of the traffic in alcoholic beverages is as wrong as it would be to defend the traffic in opiates because physicians prescribe them in certain cases.

III. FOE OF PROGRESS

1. *Statesmanship and Wine*

Julius Caesar was deeply impressed by the vigor of the Suevi, a semibarbaric people whom he encountered in Central Europe. In his *Gallic Wars* he comments at length about their prowess, physical strength, and stamina. Among other things he reports that the Suevi would not allow the importation of wine into their country, "believing it to be pernicious to the vigor both of body and of mind." It is of interest to note that Caesar, some fifty years before Christ came to earth, gave the world news of a land where strict prohibition of the use of alcoholic beverages helped to produce a sturdy type of manhood.

Plato banned alcoholic beverages from his Ideal Republic, the first great effort of man to paint a word picture of "heaven on earth." That ancient Greek philosopher knew too well the relationship between wine and human depravity to allow it a place in the state which his fertile mind sought to visualize. Lycurgus, the famous Spartan lawgiver, lived some eight hundred years before Christ and had much to do with developing the renowned Spartan race and spirit. He not only banned wine but had the vineyards that produced it destroyed. Epictetus, Greek philosopher who lived about one hundred years before Christ, although not an abstainer, admitted that danger is inherent in the use of wine and declared: "That man is a drunkard who takes more than three glasses. And though he be not drunk, he hath exceeded moderation." Hammurabi, world's greatest lawgiver except Moses, enacted prohibition statutes more than twenty-two hundred years before Christ. One restricted the employment of barmaids. It should impress the friends of the liquor traffic in this day. Other statutes controlled the production and distribution of alcoholic beverages.

2. *Mighty Greece Collapsed*

"In Greece she [Nature] accomplished the first Motherhood of Man ever presented. In the Greek, with his fair complexion, blue eyes, beautiful body and radiant face, she held aloft a gift of her abundant love. They loved liberty. Freedom had her birth among the hills of Greece. Here it was that political rights were first debated and the duties of government limited by statute." Thus does the famous historian, John Clark Ridpath, praise the early citizens of the little country in southeast Europe which may well be called the seed bed and nurturing ground of philosophy, mathematics, art, music, the physical sciences, and the birthplace of democracy.

For centuries the world has studied the writings of Greek intellectuals; military leaders have marveled at the strategy developed by Grecian officers; Greek schools and theaters have been long famed throughout the civilized world. Students of architecture and structural engineering must still study the ruins of Delphi, Athens, and other ancient cities. But too little is known about the rigid diet, exercises, and abstinence from all alcoholic beverages which produced the ancestors of the people who made ancient Greece.

And what a parade of mental giants one watches when he sees Plato in the field of political science; Aristotle, the philosopher and teacher of many geniuses; Archimedes, the great mathematician and father of all machinery using the principles of the lever; Herodotus, the father of history, and Thucydides, first in the field of historical criticism; Aeschylus, the father of tragic poetry; Pythagoras who, in spite of his religious beliefs, helped the world to realize that there is definite design in an orderly universe; Homer and his immortal Iliad; Socrates, renowned thinker, father of the dialetic (question and answer) method of teaching; Hippocrates, the father of medicine, and scores of others.

The Greeks were very religious. Paul's comment during his notable sermon on Mars Hill reveals much to one who knows the background, "In all things I perceive that ye are very religious" (Acts 17:22 asv). Unfortunately, by Paul's time priests of the various gods of the nation, creations of pagan minds, had led worshipers into many forms of debauchery, some of it too lewd to be described. As the Panhellenic empire arose to power, the idolatry increased in depravity. Consequently, the various free states were robbed of their hegemony; the small local, autonomous political units of the empire disappeared; a large per cent of the populace moved from open country and small towns into urban centers; and consumption of wine grew to large proportions. Then the situation that produced the intellectual giants was gone; Greece was ready to fall before the armies of Rome!

3. *Israel's Folly Exposed*

Time after time the Hebrews were warned about the dangers which indulgence in intoxicants produced. Although science had not discovered the narcotic nature of alcohol, and biologists had not made known its effect upon animal life, God had through his prophets revealed enough about the curse of drink for Israel to have saved herself from the degeneracy that finally brought collapse and bondage. God's messenger forbade the mother of Samson to drink wine (Judg. 13:14). As indicated already, the Nazirite had to be a total abstainer from birth (Num. 6:3). When Absalom plotted the death of his brother, he resorted to the use of wine to make him ready for slaughter (2 Sam. 13:28). A modest queen was robbed of her throne because she refused the demand of her drunken husband, Ahasuerus, to expose her lovely body before his carousing courtiers (Esther 1:10–19). While the sons and daughters of Job were engaged in feasting and drinking, the Sabeans rushed in, captured them, and slew their bodyguard (Job. 1:13–15).

Solomon saw the ravages of drink and warned against being led into error through the use of wine (Prov. 20:1). He showed how love of wine keeps one from acquiring wealth (Prov. 21:17). He painted victims of alcohol as having woe, sorrow, contentions, babblings, wounds without a cause, and redness of eyes. He urged abstinence, declaring, "At the last it biteth like a serpent, and stingeth like an adder" (Prov. 23:32). He wrote of the pitiable state of the drinker (Prov. 23:29–30). Isaiah blamed wine for Israel's downfall (5:11–13, 22–24; 22:13–14; 28:1–7). Hosea drew a gruesome picture of Israel's perfidy, connecting it with wine (Hos. 4:6–11; 7:1–6). Joel likewise blamed wine for Israel's ruin (Joel 1:5–6). He showed the relationship between drink and white slavery (Joel 3:3). Amos declared that excessive wine drinking and its accompanying debauchery would lead to captivity (Amos 6:1–7).

4. Ancient Shadows Warn America

Who can know how far alcoholic beverages have gone in undermining governments and in changing the balance of power among the nations of the world? Every nation since earliest historical records has grown great while its population was primarily rural, hence had neither time nor money with which to pay the costs involved in drinking alcoholic beverages. As Greece decayed and finally collapsed because of an urbanized population who had been demoralized by venal priests who exalted wine above all else in their worship and feasting, even so did Rome slowly degenerate. The glories of the Republic, the conquests by Caesar, the far-spread empire with its vast system of roads, the great schools, libraries, theaters and colossal athletic events—these were gradually caught in the mesh of wine. Instead of statesmen, puppets of a wicked king like Nero arose, and finally the invaders from the north caught them with no suitable defenses or defenders. Out of the scattered wreckage of the Holy Roman Empire arose the feudal states of the medieval ages which now constitute the pawns in the modern military and economic games of the great, and whose citizens continue to enslave themselves by strong drink.

Far back in time Semitic people learned of the harmful effects of alcohol. Long before man discovered what causes fermented fruit juice and moistened crushed grains to have such strange power over the human body and mind, the "mocker within the glass" had been recognized. When this was we can only infer from the fact that some of the names given wine by the forerunners of the Hebrew race were chosen because they fitted the behavior patterns of people who imbibed too freely of strong drink. Two Hebrew words show this: *yayin* whose root means to lament or wail, and *tirosh* which represents the certain trend to poverty. Proof should not be needed to convince any rational being that an alcoholic beverage is not a source of true pleasure. The revelation from history about how it undermines the will, handicaps the body, and slowly takes over the citadel and throne of the soul should be enough to turn every thoughtful ambitious person into a total abstainer.

Seeing the shadows which indulgence in alcoholic beverages has spread over the past, and with mounting evidences of its terrible hold on the modern world, one must pray with Kipling,

> Lord God of Hosts, be with us yet,
> Lest we forget—lest we forget!

SUGGESTED TOPICS FOR DISCUSSION

1. What were the restrictions under which Nazirites lived, and why were they worth observing?
2. Make a list of many references in the Old Testament in which the use of alcoholic beverages is condemned.
3. Consult your obstetrician and your pediatrician and secure from them data about the relation between alcoholism and the birth of strong, healthy children.
4. What nations not mentioned in this chapter have suffered because of the excessive use of wine?

CHAPTER 3 OUTLINE

I. BLIGHTING THE BODY
   1. The Control System
   2. A Delicate Mechanism
   3. A University Reports

II. ALCOHOL A DEPRESSANT
   1. Releasing Controls
   2. No Repairs Provided
   3. No Free Lunches
   4. Interfering with Labor

III. THE GREAT DESTROYER
   1. Abnormal Demands
   2. Barriers Removed
   3. Organs Overworked

IV. STEALING LIFE'S RESERVES
   1. The Sappers
   2. Striking at the Core
      (1) The heart
      (2) The gastro-intestinal tract
      (3) The lungs
      (4) The liver
      (5) Other organs

3

PROTECTING THE TEMPLE

In Psalm 139 David gave expression to some of the predominant emotions of the human family: wonder and fear (1–6), assurance and peace (7–12), curiosity and awe (13–16), reverence and gratitude (17–18), contempt and anger (19–22), and humility and penitence (23–24). It is significant to note that centuries before man discovered the infrared and the ultraviolet rays and other light energies invisible to the human eye, David should have written, "Even the darkness hideth not from thee, . . . the darkness and the light are both alike to thee" (Psalm 139:12 ASV).

In some ways the most striking section of this psalm is that in which David expressed the wonder and awe that gripped his heart when he considered the origin of his own body (Psalm 139:13–16). The author paraphrases these words thus: "Thou didst form my kidneys and other inner organs; thou didst knit them together, fashion into a unified system and hedge them in with the skeleton and skin, all this taking place in my mother's womb. I will continue to give thanks unto thee because thou hast made me after a fashion that causes fear and wonder. Even during the period of gestation, when I was yet an embryo in my mother's womb, I was not hidden from thee, although I was as completely shut away from man's eyes as if I had been in the heart of the earth. Furthermore, like an architect's plans for a great temple, my body had been prepared aforetime in thy great creative workshop, so that the atomic energies (unformed substance) of which I was to be made were foreseen, and even the age of the earth which I was to serve was set when yet my body was not even begun to be developed."

The human body is referred to often in the Scriptures as a temple. Jesus caused perplexity to his enemies by predicting that he would raise a thrown-down temple in three days, referring to his own body (John 2 : 21). Paul declared that the body is the temple of the Lord (1 Cor. 6:19); he mastered his own body lest it make of him a physical wreck (1 Cor. 9:27); he admonished, "Present your bodies a living sacrifice" (Rom. 12 : 1).

Since God made man after such a marvelous pattern and endowed him with the creative genius which makes him only a little inferior to the angels (Psalm 8:5), the Creator must be sorely displeased when the wonderful temple is desecrated by the imps of lust, appetite, and carnal vices! It is the solemn obligation of parents, teachers, statesmen, and ministers of religion to combine their forces to safeguard childhood and youth against the ravages of any and every evil that mars and handicaps this wonderful instrument and brings it prematurely to death's door.

I. BLIGHTING THE BODY

The wonderful medium of expression is made up of a vast assembly of nerve filaments, ganglia, and brain; of heart and arteries, capillaries and veins; of an intricate and mysterious digestive system; of blood and bones and brawn—all of them so delicately made and attuned that even microscopic particles of matter and drops of any poison can bring harm, and minute microbes and bacteria wreak havoc when once they are allowed to run loose within it. The most important physical task that confronts man, therefore, is to protect the machine by which the creative genius within, made in the image of God, may convey to the outside world visions that become visible, dreams that are made tangible, air castles that become havens for earth-bound creatures.

1. *The Control System*

The nervous system was set by the Creator to control the body, and it in turn is supposed to be controlled by the spirit or ego through the mysterious power of the will. Two tasks are set for the nervous system to perform: carrying impulses or messages to and from the brain, and directing the regular activities of the entire body. Many functions of the body go on with no conscious direction from the mind. Breathing, digestion, heart action, the secretions by glands—all are carried on from the central "control rooms" in the brain. What man should be concerned about is that all control, whether reflex or conscious, is disturbed by any little change in the normal course of life. Furthermore, these controls all center in the brain, which is easily injured. To take into the body any injurious substance is, therefore, to sin against it. Alcohol is one of the most injurious substances that can be allowed access to brain tissues, so to imbibe drinks containing it means inevitable injury to the control system. Cells within the body may repair a lesion in the skin, but they cannot do it without leaving a scar to witness to the fact that the damage was done.

2. A Delicate Mechanism

The communications system by which the mind controls the body is extremely delicate and sensitive. For example, when one touches a hot stove or suffers a pin prick, an immediate and drastic upheaval occurs at the point of contact. The sensory nerve conveys a message of danger to the brain; the alarm is sounded from it through the sensation of pain, and a motor impulse is flashed to the muscles upon which the injured member depends for safety. The injured finger is jerked away, and instantly a vast army of cells inside the blood stream is alerted and sent to repair whatever damage may have been done, while other cells throw up around the injury a protective shield from alien enemy forces which produce infection. The time required for the act of receiving the news, sending the protective response, and setting up the repair work is infinitely brief, but science can measure it and so has discovered to what extent it is disrupted by one or another form of toxic substances.

It is now a well-known fact that even a very small portion of alcohol in the blood slows down the reflexive reactions by which the safety of the body is secured. They can be temporarily but completely paralyzed by large doses of any narcotic or opiate. The muscular reflexes, which a physician tests by tapping the front of one's knees, are slowed down as much as 10 per cent by the alcohol in one stein or bottle of 5 per cent beer. The movement of the eyelid is slowed down by 6 per cent; the hand, the leg and other parts of the body may be slowed up to 60 per cent in speed of response to the brain, depending upon the amount of alcohol in the blood stream.

Since the safety of every person is dependent upon the speed and accuracy with which these reflexes operate, it behooves all people to safeguard the nervous system with jealous care. It should be as difficult to get a person to take a drink containing alcohol as it would be to get his permission to submit to a sharp blow upon the head, for both alcohol and a concussion damage the seat of reason and of life. Safety, even life itself, hangs in the balances many times each day in this age of speed and mechanization. All unknown to the healthy person, the complicated mechanism of brain, nerves, and muscles, when unimpeded, prevents disaster.

3. A University Reports

To learn how alcohol affects the nerve reflexes and thus increases the danger of accidents and death, Northwestern University's Traffic Institute made a careful and extended study, with numerous experiments. Their findings are reported in *Effects* by Rice and Harger. Taking an assumed 1 as the ratio of accidents to chances in traffic for the abstainer, they proved that .07 per cent of alcohol in the blood increases to 3 the chances of accidents; .07 to .11 per cent increases them to 5; .11 to .15 per cent to 15; above .15 per cent the chances run up to 55 to 1. In short, these studies, made scientifically, prove that the chances of accidents by a moderate drinker are from five to fifteen times greater than for the abstainer, and those of the heavy drinker as much as fifty-five times as great.[1] Any reputable physiologist or toxicologist can tell why. Alcohol so interferes with the delicate mechanism of the body that the user becomes like a ship with a

---

[1] For a summary of this study see *Effects*, by Thurman B. Rice, M.D., and Rolla N. Harger (Chicago: Wheeler, 1949), pp. 162-163.

defective rudder or a driver whose hands have become partially paralyzed.

II. ALCOHOL A DEPRESSANT

Alcohol is not a stimulant, as many people think it is, but it exercises a depressant effect upon the brain and the nervous system.

1. *Releasing Controls*

A high per cent of the brain is composed of water, and alcohol has a strong affinity for water. Within less than three minutes after the narcotic is taken into the stomach some of it has reached the brain where it robs cells of water. Immediately its functions, attention, reason, and will are modified. Likewise the area of the brain from which reflexes arise is affected. In proportion to the amount of alcohol in the blood and the degree of immunity that has already been built up against it, so will be the extent to which these functions are impeded.

Dr. Haven Emerson calls attention to the crippling influence of alcohol. One may, he asserts, find freedom from timidity, worry, fear, and such, by taking alcoholic beverages, but the freedom is thus won "through sacrifice of a correct functioning of the higher faculties of judgment, discretion, and self-control." He adds, "Sensory and motor functions are all slowed, rendered less accurate, and lack customary endurance." And that is not all he warns against. "Excitement and increase of activity following the taking of alcohol are not due to a stimulant action but to unchecked response to emotional situations." [2] It is, therefore, very unwise for anyone to allow

[2] Haven Emerson, M.D., *Alcohol: Its Effects on Man* (New York: D. Appleton Century, 1936), pp. 31-32.

himself, for the sake of temporary relief from some complex or some emotional situation to pour into his system the narcotic which he must receive whenever he drinks a beverage containing alcohol. What good is the temporary relief, the momentary pleasure, the freedom from worry, when they are gained at the expense of destroying the very body that one must use in life's big game?

2. *No Repairs Provided*

"A real food promotes muscular, glandular, and nerve activity, and its oxidation maintains the bodily temperature. But alcohol disturbs muscular, glandular, and nerve activity, and its oxidation does not maintain bodily heat." Thus does an authoritative work present a basic fact with which medical science has long been familiar. Dr. Haven Emerson declares, "Although a substance may provide heat or energy for the body, if it cannot serve to repair or build tissue or if it cannot be stored in the body for subsequent use when needed, it is not ordinarily thought of as a food." [3] He named three classes of foods: substances which provide energy and materials for repairs and the growth of tissues, such as albuminous or meaty foods; fuels which provide heat and can also be stored, such as fats and carbohydrates; fuels that provide temporary heat but neither repair nor are stored.

Alcohol is the one substance which meets the third classification. He says of it, "Alcohol can take no part in the creation, growth, building, or repair functions of foods." [4] No argument for alcohol as an item of food is valid. To substitute it for fats and carbohydrates is to load the system with a fuel that spurs to activity but

[3] *Ibid.*, p. 7.
[4] *Ibid.*, p. 8.

hastens the wear and destruction of the body. Ultimately the use of this fictitious food element will bring complete collapse of the body—death!

3. *No Free Lunches*

The old-time liquor store often gave a free lunch with a stein of beer. The bartender never thought of the beverage as a food; it was only an alcoholic liquor sold for the benefit of the makers and vendors. Alcoholic beverages never give one a store of food. As far as their food value goes, it is limited to temporary heat caused by the oxidation produced in the effort of the body to be rid of the substance against which by nature it rebels. Only in special cases which an honest physician determines should it ever be substituted for true foods. It is never included in the diet list for children. Any coach who would require an alcoholic beverage to be substituted for milk and water on a training table would be fired by college authorities or else would turn out a team of losers. The businessman, the housekeeper, the laborer, and all others should realize that they are members of the great social, economic, and political team upon whose efficiency is dependent the welfare of the nation, including the well-being of their own homes and individual lives. Alcoholic beverages should, therefore, have no place on the dining tables of the land, no part in the diet list of a free people.

4. *Interfering with Labor*

Every movement of the limbs, every batting of an eye, every throb of the heart, every contraction of any muscle, require energy which can only be had in an ample and regular supply when the digestive system is in good condition and assimilation is unhampered. Every breath one draws, every step he takes, every idea which his mind formulates in the brain—every effort which is a part of living causes destruction of cells in the body. Furthermore, health and strength and happiness are dependent upon the system of elimination whereby waste materials in the food are expelled from the body and the "ashes of burned out cells and fumes from the oxidation of fuels" are carted out of the system. Inside the body there is an intricate workshop in which microscopic laborers are ever busy at the task of repairing the damage which expenditure of energy always causes, and of carting away all rubbish left from their work. Wisdom will lead everyone whom she directs so to govern himself that both the repair and the cleansing functions be not compelled to do useless labor in taking care of any substance not required in their fields.

III. THE GREAT DESTROYER

There was an awful suspense during World War I when the German Big Bertha was lobbing bombs into Paris from a distance of sixty miles, when France had her back to the wall, and her soldiers maintained their mental poise by crying, "They shall not pass!" England had been bled white and American doughboys, now called G.I.'s, were being rushed, many only partly trained, into slaughter on the western front. The Argonne, Belleau Wood, Verdun, and Amiens are familiar names to veterans of those terrifying days which saw relatives throughout the world watching the bulletins daily to see what new casualties would be reported.

In those days frantic appeals were made to civilians for increased production of war goods, for holding down consumption of strategic foods, and for the elimination of every possible waste. "Win the war" was the dominant desire in every heart, the driving motive of citizens everywhere. Everything that could impede progress overseas or in any way interfere with the operation of the war machine was turned aside. Production and transportation, backed by conservation on every hand, provided the means whereby the tides of battle were turned.

In the program by which success was brought to the allied armies both in 1918 and in 1945, one finds a striking parallel to the regimen that will bring victory in the human struggle against the invisible hordes of enemy forces forever attacking the flesh. Just as production and distribution of supplies made for a victorious fighting force, even so do the regular functions inside the body make for healthy, happy living which, in turn, enables anyone to be a vital, dynamic member of society. Since the digestive system must produce and the circulatory system transport all materials needed in the battle of life, and the nervous system is the governing and directing agency, it behooves everyone to know that whatever temporary pleasure he may gain from alcoholic beverages is secured at the risk of ultimate defeat in the struggle to survive. Everyone should look at the drink problem with this in mind.

1. *Abnormal Demands*

King Alcohol is a stern taskmaster. Wherever he gains control he makes himself a tzar. Even when taken in moderation he slowly develops such a place for himself that thousands of his followers come to be his abject slaves. Once established inside the body of any subject, the effort to oust him brings an extreme emotional upset which the poor subject is rarely willing to endure, so remains in bondage. The subject may die, but "Long Live King Alcohol!" becomes his slogan.

Nature's foods never create this abnormal demand for themselves. The appetite repeatedly calls for food, but it does not demand one certain kind of bread and that alone. One kind of meat may be substituted for another at any meal and the emotional balance remain unaffected. One may eat whole wheat toast every morning for a month and find on the first morning of the next month that biscuits or rolls constitute a delightful variation in the diet. But it is not so with mixtures containing alcohol. If one takes regularly an alcoholic beverage, regardless of its kind, before long the craving for the narcotic in it will become so dominant that, if it is omitted, a rebellion arises inside. The more potent the narcotic the more violent the emotional upset caused when it is left out. The panic that seizes an alcoholic when no more liquor is in sight furnishes an inescapable indictment of all who turn from the regular sources of nourishment to indulge in dangerous, deadly substitutes.

2. *Barriers Removed*

A second cause of damage which users of alcohol incur is the slow breakdown of inhibitions which nature has set up for the protection of all animal forms. As *Death Loses the Game* points out, an occasional child develops an abnormal desire for dirt; a person can become an addict to quinine; a lovely girl endangers her life because of a craving for salted vinegar.[5] Every such appetite is a source of danger and premature death unless brought

---

[5] John D. Freeman, *Death Loses the Game* (Chicago: Moody Press, 1954).

under control. Some people become gluttons; others become slaves to caffein or nicotine, and a few to opiates. But there is no psychological difference between the dirt eater and the user of a narcotic or an opiate; each is the unfortunate victim of a perverted appetite because he overrode the natural barriers against such excesses. The more powerful the objectionable element of diet in its attack upon the nervous system, the more immediate and complete the slavery into which it leads.

The unfortunate thing about any breach of the barriers which nature set up to protect animal life from useless and harmful substitutes for food and drink lies in the fact that, once the substitute gets a foothold, it not only demands more room for itself but brings in its allies. Thus the dirt eater comes to crave narcotics, the user of narcotics begins to demand opiates, and in the end complete slavery is the result of allowing the abnormal desire ever to be tolerated.

With any alcoholic beverage the course runs the same. The temporary pleasure which the drink brings to the user is had while extra tissues which it cannot replace are being consumed. An extra amount of carbon dioxide is produced which the alcohol cannot help remove from the body. Because it cannot rebuild or restore tissues, it creates an extra need for real food while, at the same time, removing the inhibitions against overeating and the ability to select correct articles of diet. In the end the drinker becomes the victim of a distressing form of nausea.

3. Organs Overworked

Alcohol causes some of the glands and organs of the body to be overworked. For example, the tear ducts are irritated by the presence of alcohol in the blood, so bedimmed eyes and overflowing tears mark one partly intoxicated. The increased activity of the kidneys after one has drunk a bottle or two of beer is due not only to the effort to rid the body of the surplus water, but to the effort to help expel the alcohol from the blood. The pancreas and the spleen likewise are forced to do extra work because of the alcohol.

So, to consume alcoholic beverages means to put upon the delicate machinery of the body useless labor. It also hastens the day when that body will be impaired and parts of it ruined beyond repair. Certainly one would not expect a motor to go on operating when valves are corroded or destroyed, feed lines choked with trash, and the ignition system disrupted by faulty wires and a crippled power plant. How then can he hope to have a strong, energetic, well-controlled body when he allows alcohol to damage vital glands and organs, cripple the brain, and weaken the nerves?

IV. Stealing Life's Reserves

One of the most important departments of a modern army is the intelligence corps, that group of enlisted men and officers whose business it is to safeguard all of the command by keeping in touch with the enemy, anticipating his movements, and alerting each group of fighting men when it is endangered by what the enemy plans to do. When the intelligence corps is in good hands and alert, the danger of surprise attack is greatly reduced. Anything that saps its strength or lessens the acuteness of the perception upon which it is dependent also puts in jeopardy the army which it serves. Since the nervous system constitutes the Intelligence Corps of the human body, there is every reason to safeguard it against whatever interferes with its free and full functioning. Alcohol is an enemy which it must always watch.

1. *The Sappers*

The brain is the center of the nervous system, the agent to which all information must go, wherein all decisions must be made, and from which all communications must be sent. Anything that interferes with the regular functions of the brain is, therefore, a source of danger to the entire body. Sappers are employed by any army for the purpose of undermining the strength of the enemy, so whoever would overthrow manhood and womanhood must strike at the sources of power within the body. See how mental sappers work.

Overwork and worry constitute a pair of sappers against which many an unfortunate person has to wage warfare. Overwork wears out the tissues faster than they can be replaced. If worry continues, it weakens the source of reason, diverts mental energy from useful ends, consumes brain cells to no purpose, and gradually develops some worse form of mental illness, a neurosis or a psychosis which allows various phobias to plague the victim and sometimes drive him to suicide.

The use of alcohol likewise injures the brain. This it does by robbing it of its precious water, interfering with the regular functions of the will, and robbing it of the power to control all bodily functions. While worry wears down the nervous system and ultimately brings serious disorders to the brain, alcohol is far worse for it not only weakens the brain cells but also opens the door to a whole bevy of evils.

For anyone, therefore, to seek escape from petty worries and distressing complexes by resorting to alcoholic beverages or opiates is an admission of personal weakness or inferiority as a human being, and hence is far from being a mark of the gentility which the friends of such beverages try to persuade mankind that moderate drinking indicates. One may use alcohol as an "escape medium" by which to gain temporary release from trouble, but the escape thus gained is that of the prisoner who walks from the dining room across a sunlit courtyard to his cell. He who would keep the "intelligence corps" virile and ever alert and active must battle against alcohol and all other substances which undermine the centers from which rational as well as physical existence come.

2. Striking at the Core

(1) *The heart.*—A Negro sage once said, "No, Suh, I ain' afeard of what a ghos' may do to me; what bothers me is what he will make me do to myself." So, when the friends of legalized liquor speak about the harmless effects of alcohol upon the muscles of the heart, they ignore the trouble. Alcohol does not materially damage muscle fibers; what it does to injure the heart is, as already pointed out, to remove the restraining hands of the nerve control so that the heart runs away. Furthermore, it tends to dilate the blood vessels which in turn release pressure upon the blood and thus speed up the pulse. So the heart, affected by alcohol, speeds up its work about 10 per cent and, of course, cannot operate as many years as nature intended it to.

(2) *The gastro-intestinal tract.*—The flow of saliva, bile, gastric, and pancreatic juices, is usually quickened by the first small quantity of alcohol swallowed, but the increased flow is of an inferior quality. The gastric juice contains less pepsin. After repeated doses of alcohol, the

flow is decreased and the quality remains inferior. So the regular user of alcohol, even in moderate amounts, is quite often an easy victim of the seller of patent nostrums which are "guaranteed to relieve acid indigestion and the unpleasant fulness in the abdomen." The continued use of alcoholic beverages so irritates the membranes of the digestive tract that they secrete a mucous which further interferes with digestion.

(3) *The lungs.*—One vital function of the lungs is to discharge from the blood stream carbon dioxide and other such waste matter. Alcohol provides only heat and in being converted into heat generates extra carbon dioxide. Only a very small proportion of alcohol is thrown off by skin and kidneys; the wear of the lung tissues caused by the alcohol is, therefore, much greater, makes them susceptible to pneumonia and other pulmonary diseases, and causes these diseases to be fatal in far more cases than where they strike total abstainers.

(4) *The liver.*—The effect of alcohol upon the liver has long been debated by scientists. But the proof definitely connects cirrhosis of the liver with the use of alcohol. Dr. C. C. Weeks of England found that it produced from 5 to 13 per cent of deaths from this cause in the British Isles.

(5) *Other organs.*—Alcohol does not materially affect the tissues of the eye, the ear, or even the nerves that serve under the skin. But again it is not what the drug does to the tissue, but what it releases the tissue to do to itself. So the eye is made less responsive to stimuli. Small quantities of alcohol slow down its response as much as 10 per cent. Larger doses destroy its power to focus accurately, so the drinker sees double; he often sees things that do not exist outside his brain.

Mining engineers know what it means to try to make a profit from ores that are too low in mineral content. Around Cripple Creek, Colorado, and many another once famous mining center, one sees the rotting remains of smelters, shaft housings, and tipples. Why were they abandoned? Because the cost of smelting the ore outran the value of the precious metals taken from it. When will mankind learn that the excessive cost of what little heat and excitement anyone may secure from alcoholic beverages far exceeds any value he may receive from them? To argue that the manufacture and sale of alcoholic beverages should not be rigidly controlled because they contain a modicum of fuel-food is like arguing that rattlers should not be removed from the streets because their venom provides relief from rheumatism.

SUGGESTED TOPICS FOR DISCUSSION

1. Visit the police or the sheriff's headquarters and check the number of arrests for any given month, and the number of these in which alcohol caused or helped cause the arrest.
2. Ask your family physician for a list of diseases he could not successfully treat without alcohol.
3. Check with the employers of your community—a few of the many in the city—and see who of them will employ a known user of alcohol. See if the liquor store owner hires any of the alcoholics he has helped produce!

CHAPTER 4 OUTLINE

I. FALLACIOUS CLAIMS

    1. Either an Alcoholic or Else!

    2. Do Wise People Drink?

    3. Relief from Restraints

    4. Special Occasions Demand Alcoholic Drinks

    5. Control Whets Appetites

II. CHARACTER CRUSHED

    1. Fear Complex Deadened

    2. Pride Falls Down

    3. Eyes Are Dimmed

III. TIME TO WORRY

    1. Social Restraints Broken

    2. Religious Restraints Removed

    3. The Mating Instinct Marred

4

REMOVING THE MASK

It was a brilliant occasion, so the story of other days went. The cream of society's elite had gathered in the palatial home of a prominent couple for the annual masquerade ball. No expense had been spared in providing decorations, food, and music for the evening. Costumes ran all the way from a facsimile of a queen's coronation gown to a hobo's ragged garb.

The guest who wore the hobo's clothes was indeed a vagrant. He had found a ticket to the ball and had dared to attend because he felt that the mask over his face would shield him from detection. He had known better days before alcohol had made a vagabond of him. He danced well and knew many things expected of a guest in such a group. But one thing he did not know; at midnight all masks had to be removed!

When the hour came and he was compelled to uncover, the hosts were astonished to see the bearded, unkempt face of an impostor whose ragged clothes were all he had on. Ladies who had danced with him were humiliated; their escorts were furious. The hobo was thrust from the house, an angry interloper who had enjoyed for a brief time a popularity which he in no wise merited.

There is another masquerader which today is enjoying popularity at almost every social affair among the elite, and he attends social functions among the middle class and the poor. But the mask is being removed; his pretentious claims are being exposed as false; his hold upon certain influential groups of citizens is being lost; the time is here when Mr. Alcoholic Beverages will be unmasked and revealed for what he by nature is and always has been, a mocker who deceives by subtlety, a tyrant who enslaves by degrees and destroys with no regard for one's culture or social standing. It is time for the unmasking to be hastened.

I. FALLACIOUS CLAIMS

Prior to the days of the Eighteenth Amendment the liquor store was called a saloon and was the known ally of gambling, crooked politics, and prostitution, and a breeder of crime. Its victims were called drunks or sots and were ostracized by reputable social groups. But shrewd propaganda has changed the attitude of the public. Now it is "genteel to drink, and moderation in the use of alcoholic beverages is a mark of good breeding." The saloon is now a mixing bar, the beer garden a tavern, and the drunkard must be treated at public expense because he is sick! Ready-made excuses for drinking beverage alcohol are turned out monthly by brewers, distillers, and vintners. Real artists, directed by skilled propagandists, are paid to bombard the eyes and the ears of the citizenry with their deceptive, fallacious, and often insidious claims which an unwitting public all too frequently accepts without question.

Offering excuses for sin is as old as the race. The displeasure of God at the fall of man in Eden was answered by Eve with the honest statement, "The serpent beguiled me, and I did eat." But Adam resorted to a subterfuge and answered his Maker, "The woman whom thou gavest to be with me, she gave me of the tree, and I did eat" (Gen. 3:12 asv). The liquor industry has taken advantage of this tendency of mankind to "follow the leader," so "everybody drinks" is now one of its slogans; and "if you want to be genteel, learn how to drink as a lady and a gentleman should" is a deceptive lure which is causing hosts of people voluntarily to subject themselves to the danger of becoming addicts. But no propaganda can denature the alcohol. "At the last it biteth like a serpent, and stingeth like an adder" (Prov. 23:32).

A Negro was once accused by his pastor of indulging in the use of liquor, whereupon he replied, "Well, Suh, I admits dat I takes a toddy now and then, but I ain't never drunk to success." Inadvertently he expressed a great truth for, regardless of how little or how much alcohol one may consume, it never contributes to his success in any worthy endeavor. A wise person will, therefore, study the claims of the liquor and beer manufacturers and learn how subtle and alluring but how erroneous and misleading they are.

1. *Either an Alcoholic or Else!*

In 1873, Dr. Henry I. Bowditch of Massachusetts advanced the hypothesis that certain cosmic laws determine whether one will be an alcoholic or not. His theory was akin to that which claims that if one is unfortunate enough to be born under the wrong astrological setup he will be unable to resist the lure of strong drink. But neither fatalistic theory has been able to dispose of the fact that in 1873 only one of every 60 people born under any constellation became an alcoholic, while in 1955 the United States produced one alcoholic for every 28 people, regardless of when they were born.

A woman contributor to a newspaper expressed another current fatalistic claim: "People are alcoholics because of inherent weaknesses; if they were not alcoholics, they might be something worse." Thus goes the effort to put blame for the distressing effects of strong drink upon everything except the real culprit, the liquor industry itself. The plain truth is that the more than four and a half million alcoholics in the United States at the close of 1955, two-thirds of them chronic cases, endure their pitiable condition because society makes alcoholic beverages available to them and protects makers and vendors of these beverages while they continue to place before the public the narcotic which weakens the source of all rational existence, the brain.

If one accepts as valid such claims as those of Dr. Bowditch and the woman writer to the newspaper, he gives valuable testimony in support of the claims of abstainers; for, whether society admits it or not, the state was ordained of God for the protection and welfare of all citizens (Rom. 13:7), not to provide legal sanction under which a very small minority may carry on the manufacture and sale of beverages which enslave so many. Civilized man has always recognized his obligation to care for the weak and the underprivileged of his race. Even barbarians have acknowledged this obligation!

Strange indeed is a statesmanship which assumes that because some people are weaklings by nature they should be left to be prey for others who, knowing that the weaknesses exist, use them for the purpose of making fat profits by selling harmful goods. Many people will express their weaknesses through some form of evil, but it is far more wicked to induce them to drink alcoholic beverages upon the ground that it is better for such people to become alcoholics, since otherwise they would probably be something worse. Furthermore, it is a gullible statesman who can be hoodwinked by such a claim and thus be led to legalize the trade in alcoholic beverages. Alcoholics come from every class of citizens. They are made by the narcotic drug which is found in all brands of beers, ales, wines, and distilled spirits, and which is no respecter of persons.

2. *Do Wise People Drink?*

"It's smart to drink" is often said by makers and sellers of alcoholic beverages. Movie screens have been used for decades to present drinking scenes in which social groups are shown at elaborate banquets, in beautiful living rooms, on shipboard, at picnics, or elsewhere with their wine, beer, or social cocktails much in evidence. Television now takes such scenes into millions of homes, where little ones are led to look upon beer and wine as absolute essentials to well-being. An ever-increasing number of parents are seduced by the alluring propaganda. The ultimate effect of this type of publicity, aided and abetted by color advertising in newspapers and magazines, will be to produce a nation of alcoholics who will be helpless to withstand any death-dealing epidemic or an invasion by armed forces from a sober nation. It is not smart to drink alcoholic beverages; it is extremely stupid, for one of every nine drinkers is doomed to become either an alcoholic or a problem drinker.

3. *Relief from Restraints*

"A bit of alcohol helps me with my guests," says a thoughtless host. "A nip at the right time peps me up and I forget to be timid," says an aspiring social climber. To resort to the use of alcoholic beverages in order to limber up a party or to overcome timidity is to admit that one is of an inferior character, lacking in initiative, and deficient in ability to do constructive thinking. Racing commissions have enacted rigid rules with heavy penalties against making race horses helpless victims of dope injections before they run on the track. Why should rational beings resort to a shot of alcohol in order to overcome any social handicap? To drink any alcoholic beverage is not to be genteel but to be extremely gullible.

The late Dr. Robert V. Seliger, in his booklet *It's Smarter Not to Drink* sets forth some of the penalties one incurs by being a social drinker. It breaks the ice at a party, he admits, but also breaks down judgment; it loosens the timid tongue, but removes the mental brakes so that all too often the drinker talks too much; it enlivens a party, but it also dulls the mind so that drinkers, especially women, are far more apt to have part in sex indiscretions. He denies that alcohol is needed as a medicine and concludes, "The so-called 'assets' of social drinking are few and questionable, while the liabilities definitely point toward hazard or danger and include the serious reality that every alcoholic was once, presumably, a 'social drinker'." [1]

4. *Special Occasions Demand Alcoholic Drinks*

Since time immemorial some people have believed that alcoholic beverages should be used during certain special occasions, such as banquets, weddings, and birthdays. Wine has also been used in connection with religious rites, and rarely has its use been limited to the small

---

[1] Robert V. Seliger, M.D., *It's Smarter Not to Drink* (Columbus, Ohio: School and College Service, 1953), p. 26.

amount needed at altars. Dr. Charles B. Towns, noted specialist in the treatment of drug addicts, wrote a telling appeal for legislation that would protect the weak of society against the wolves who make their profits by catering to the human desire for relief from pain and worry, or the never satisfied desire for temporal pleasure. He begins chapter 7 thus: "Alcoholics are more easily classified than drug-takers. With few exceptions, alcohol-users have their beginnings in social drinking."

Why should one not say no when asked to take a drink? To submit when common sense bids him refuse is a mark of great inferiority, never an evidence of smartness. Chocolate causes some people to suffer violent attacks of sinusitis; one who has this allergy would be stupid to eat a piece of chocolate pie because the hostess set it before him at dinner. A party that cannot get going without resorting to beer or wine or cocktails is a poor excuse for entertainment. A birthday that cannot be celebrated without the use of intoxicants is an anniversary that should be ignored. A host or hostess who cannot entertain without muddling the minds of guests with alcohol gives definite proof of a weak personality.

5. Control Whets Appetites

"If you do not have legalized liquors, you will make people want all the more to drink, and the traffic in bootlegging will overwhelm the nation with illicit intoxicants of a low and damaging grade." This is another claim of the liquor industry which has swept hosts of church members into the wet column on election days.

The liquor industry adopted after 1919 a pattern of propaganda evidently developed for them by skilled psychologists, that is, to repeat certain statements until they become a part of the thought pattern of the public. Present an idea in enough different ways, in enough different places, and by enough different media, and it will become a mental complex in people. This is exactly how so many American people have come to be so friendly toward the beverage alcohol business. The subtlety of this "psychological warfare" is detected by few people, hence hosts of them fall into the trap and become both patrons of the business and staunch opponents of any effort to control it.

Every sensible person knows that the use of any commodity is not increased by removing it from the counters and by refusing to allow it to be advertised. For what end does the liquor industry spend some quarter billion dollars per year for advertising in newspapers, magazines, and over the air, if prohibitory laws increase consumption of their products? Close every avenue of publicity to the liquor industry—radio, television, press, billboards, and the United States mails—and within a year the sales of beer, wine, and other intoxicants will drop by 20 per cent. Put all alcoholic beverages in the same category as kindred drugs—morphine, cocaine, and heroin—and keep as close watch over their production and distribution as is kept over the opiates. Create propaganda that will cause society to consider the moonshiner and the bootlegger as depraved criminals as the dope peddler now is and hunt them down as the sellers of dope are being hunted today; then within a generation an alcoholic will be as rare a person as the dope addict is today.

II. CHARACTER CRUSHED

Sixty and more years ago Henry Love owned and operated a gin and grist mill at Oak Hill, Arkansas. For years Walter Curry ran the steam engine which pulled the machinery. This was the first steam engine the author ever saw, and memories of the fascination which it came to have for him are still vivid. On one occasion Mr. Curry induced the timid country boy to enter the engine room and there explained to him a bit about what made "the wheels go round." Among other things he told how the governor balls, atop the engine and connected with it by small pulleys and a belt, controlled the speed of the big flywheel whose great belt pulled the gins and press above. "When the pressure starts up," he said, "the engine goes faster. But the governor balls are forced upward by being turned faster and they lift a valve which shuts off some of the steam. As long as that do-dad is operating, I have no fear of the engine's running wild, or of the boiler's exploding. You see, if the Bogan Mill near Mineola had been equipped with this safety device, the explosion a few weeks ago that killed two men would not have occurred."

The funeral at Bethesda Baptist Church and the burial of the two explosion victims were still fresh in the lad's mind, for school was held in the church house and had to be dismissed for the occasion and, of course, all the pupils attended both the service and the interment in the near-by graveyard. So memories of the little "governor" abide. The balls on small metal arms whirling around a central stem and moving up by centrifugal force so as to close the valve and reduce the power have furnished a perfect illustration of the safety reflexes the Creator put within all living forms. Only man who can reason goes against the instinctive restraints such as fear and pride and makes himself a slave of evils against which they would safeguard him. How are they broken down?

1. *Fear Complex Deadened*

Bashfulness, timidity, and all related emotional disturbances grow out of the fear instinct which is a part of the equipment upon which survival of all flesh is largely dependent. This reflex can be overcome. The fearful dog that would bite at one's sudden effort to pat his head can readily be led to wag his tail in ecstasy over any slight attention. The baby that will scream in terror if a strange face is suddenly thrust before his eyes will soon nestle in the arms below that face and coo with delight. The timid swain can drive himself into the presence of the fair ladies and gradually the fear complex will give way.

But the fear complex will give way also to things that damage and ruin. Fear of becoming drunk will disappear with one or two drinks of an alcoholic beverage. Fear of what society will think about one's conduct will break down before repeated sins against society. Fear of future ruin and disgrace which alcohol so often brings to its user will break down before the desire for social prestige, and when the dreaded result has come one will be helpless to recover himself from the curse that enslaved him.

Especially tragic is the breakdown of fear of what illicit sex relations will cause. Drs. Thurman B. Rice and Rolla N. Harger have issued a serious warning to women who have been tempted to drink, even in moderation. The breakdown of restraint, even by moderate drinking, is, they say "particularly dangerous where it bears on the sexual relations between unmarried persons. A woman who is ordinarily chaste . . . is far more prone to give consent to conduct which may greatly embarrass her. . . .

By no means should a young woman take even a small drink, if she is with a man who may wish to take advantage of her weakened resistence." [2]

2. *Pride Falls Down*

"Pluck the plumes from a peacock's tail and you break his heart," is a well-known adage in places where peafowls are raised. The gorgeous bird has long been the symbol of unholy pride. But the peacock is not the only creature which the Creator endowed with pride nor the only one greatly harmed when that trait is crushed. Pride is found throughout the animal world. This instinct is a needed safeguard for any normal person. It *does* matter what others may think unless one has sunk so low that pride is dead! Foolish parents sometimes humiliate a little boy for boasting about what "I'm goin' to be when I get growed up." Football stars weep unashamed when they make errors that are costly. A parent's humiliation is distressing when a child becomes a prodigal. But of all the cases of wounded pride the author has ever known, the alcoholic is the most pitiable. Scores of them have, in abject gloom, sought escape from the sense of utter depravity and complete shame into which strong drink has taken them. "Pride goeth before destruction, and an haughty spirit before a fall" (Prov. 16:18). It does this, however, only when it leads one to become a snob or to ignore advice from his true friends. It will allow one to fall whenever he becomes the victim of alcohol.

3. *Eyes Are Dimmed*

> Vice is a monster of so frightful mien
> That to be hated needs but to be seen;

---

[2] Rice and Harger, *Effects* (Chicago: Wheeler, 1949), p. 112.

> But seen too oft, familiar with her face,
> We first endure, then pity, then embrace.

No truer picture of the steps by which one becomes an alcoholic can be found than these words from Pope's "An Essay on Man." The conversion from revulsion to tolerance, then to defending and finally to acceptance marks the life of every victim of strong drink. "If I thought I would ever be as stupid as Mary was last night at the class party, I'd never touch another drop of liquor" said a high school girl one morning after. The following year she and Mary were sent home from the class party because they became intoxicated. Social drinking had led her to embrace what she despised a year before.

Sirens employed today by the liquor industry to seduce unwary people are the billboard, flaunting before the public the modern home with beer bottles showing inside an open refrigerator; the gentlemen's club with a bottle of bourbon on the table; the wonderful array of color advertising in the slick magazines; the partly nude car hops who wait upon the parked customers of the tavern; the expensive furnishings and the dreamy lighting in the club, the roadhouse, the tavern, and the cabaret; and the glittering array of lovely bottles in the liquor store. An evidence of the low state to which the industry has sunk is seen in the Christmas holidays advertisements using pictures of the Christ child, as well as of the Madonna and other Bible characters, displayed along with the urge to drink. They all glitter like gold, but what cheap tinsel they turn out to be!

III. TIME TO WORRY

"It's your worry!" is a subhead of an article in *Pageant*. It is followed by the statement, "Don't worry about the alcoholics. You are the one in danger—whether you drink three times a day, once a week or only to celebrate a wedding once a year. Alcohol damage can't be repaired." On the same page is a statement given in answer to the question, Why worry? "Why?" it asks; *"Because every time you take a drink you die a little."* Then the explanation, "Although the body has great regenerative powers, the cells of the brain and nervous system, once destroyed, are lost forever—and we know these are the cells affected, first and most potently, by C_2H_5OH, ethyl alcohol." [3]

1. *Social Restraints Broken*

"Thou shalt not steal" is a part of the constitution of the moral universe. Even barbarians have unwritten laws against violation of this commandment of which they never heard. But a few drinks of alcohol bring one to regard property rights as unimportant. A large per cent of burglaries are traced to users of alcohol. A few months of heavy drinking will make one steal in order to gratify his craving for drink.

"Thou shalt not bear false witness against thy neighbor" is another part of the moral code. The "tattletale" has long been the object of scorn, and the loose-tongued citizen the source of danger to his country during war. But let the most discreet person come under the influence of alcohol and see where the safeguard against loose talk goes. Falsehoods are resorted to in the effort to furnish an excuse for the sorry state into which drink turns him.

2. *Religious Restraints Removed*

The greatest ally of the beverage alcohol traffic in past ages has been the forces of religion. As pointed out in

---

[3] *Pageant,* Feb., 1956, pp. 151-152.

chapter 2, wine and the altar have been inseparable, while rites that require much wine have too often been associated with lewdness in conduct. To know to what depths of depravity alcoholic beverages have carried prelates of Christian churches, one should read an unabridged edition of the autobiography of Benvenuto Cellini, the famous Italian sculptor and goldsmith. Or go to "Canterbury Tales," by Geoffrey Chaucer. In an unabridged edition of this story the moral filth of the age is peddled while pilgrims, including the priest, go leisurely on their way to worship at a shrine in Canterbury.

Religion, if it is worthy of its name, should impel mankind to control all instinctive reactions of his flesh to its environment. Natural desires—like appetite, the gregarious, the acquisitive, and the procreative urges—all must be controlled, else they are turned to lust, and James tells us that lust is the mother of sin, and sin when full-grown brings forth death (James 1:14-15 marg.). Alcohol removes restraints upon natural impulses and converts them into lust, for it weakens the mental control over them. The story of the priest who was caught by revelers and given his choice of doing one of three sins bears out the claim. He was told he must either get drunk, spend the night at gambling, or visit a house of prostitution. He chose the first as being the least offensive and became drunk. When morning came he found he had lost all his money at a gaming house and had visited a house of ill fame. All moral restraints disappear when alcohol takes over the seat of the mind and will!

3. *The Mating Instinct Marred*

The battle against polygamy has been waged through long centuries. From Solomon, with the most elaborate harem ever known, all the way to the pagan chief in an African jungle with five or ten wives, the tendency of man to yield to the sex urge through numerous wives has been witnessed. Today it is being seen in Christian lands in the multiple marriages which a citizen is permitted to enter into by the divorce courts. The nation that outlawed polygamy in Utah allows every state to make legitimate any number of wives or husbands, provided only one is kept at a time. That alcohol is a chief factor in turning husbands and wives to the divorce mills is shown by any court handling divorce cases. A news release stated: "The most recent American Institute of Public Opinion survey finds that the *third* most frequent source of family quarrels in the United States is drinking." Thus the noted Gallup Poll uncovers one serious ground for fear of the ultimate consequences of alcoholic beverages upon national welfare.

Let no one be deceived by the propaganda of the liquor industry. It is not smart to drink; it is extremely silly! It is not genteel to indulge moderately under the assumption that one is immune to the alcoholic complex; that is to be extremely gullible. It is not a mark of good breeding to offer alcoholic beverages to guests; it indicates a deficiency in cultural graces.

SUGGESTED TOPICS FOR DISCUSSION

1. Make a list of arguments which pro-liquor forces of your community present against liquor control.
2. Check the divorce court files and see how many suits are on record in which alcohol was involved.
3. Make a list of evil effects which you know arose out of drinking on special social or religious occasions.

CHAPTER 5 OUTLINE

I. WHERE SHADOWS THICKEN
   1. A Free Citizenry
   2. A Dominant Hope
   3. Unswerving Loyalty
   4. Cases in Court
   5. A Poet's Warning

II. MENACING MANHOOD
   1. By Handicapped Citizens
   2. What About the Future?

III. BURDENING GOOD BACKS
   1. Increasing Tax Load
   2. Declining Safety Margin
   3. Our Complex Society
   4. Death or Else

5

SHADOWS ARE GATHERING

"WE's gwine have a storm befo' night. I feels it in my bones, an' de critters done sensed it comin'."

Thus did Uncle Luke, Negro sage of Burke Township, often deliver a warning when the day's work was about to begin on the farm. Rarely did he miss a prediction for he had been born in an African jungle and was in his early teens before being caught by slave traders and brought to the United States. His natural sensitiveness to weather conditions had remained with him. His neighbors, both white and black, paid special attention to his forecasts.

Social revolutions are like sudden and violent disturbances in the weather. A sociologist senses their approach years in advance of the time when the full fury breaks. Prophets issue their warnings; wise students of history point out trends that are ominous. Isaiahs, Jeremiahs, and Hoseas warn the thoughtless populace about the disaster which they are bringing upon themselves by their heedless disregard of the laws of God. Long before the evolution of human society was analyzed and the definite laws controlling it were discovered, God's prophets were inspired to know the relation between certain social trends and cataclysmic upheavals within the social body or overwhelming oppression from without. Thus they were impelled to seek to save people from the ruinous culmination of their heedless disregard of individual and corporate acts.

Shadows are gathering over the civilized world; already they have covered many nations and the wreckage of revolutionary changes may be seen in social, political, industrial, and religious circles. The clouds approach America; under cover of an inflated economy evil forces are working. The lust for carnal pleasure and the passion to gain riches cast a deepening pall across the land. Let not the eyes of students become so adjusted to the slowly gathering darkness that they will ignore the storm which it forebodes.

I. WHERE SHADOWS THICKEN

Three factors are essential to the well-being and security of any social body, especially of any state: a free citizenry, a dominant hope, and unswerving loyalty. All men are created to be free, but real freedom is inseparably connected with ownership of the soil. No one can be an enthusiastic and highly profitable citizen who cannot look to the future without fear because he sees his liberty protected and ever before him the assurance of security and personal well-being. The citizen who loses love for and loyalty to the social group of which he is a part soon becomes a liability to that group. He it is who is ever ready to espouse the cause of any ambitious rogue who advocates the overthrow of the existing order and the substitution for it of some utopian scheme which inflamed minds readily conceive or accept. Look at these factors as being affected by the gigantic traffic in alcoholic beverages and one of any degree of statesmanship will be alarmed.

1. A Free Citizenry

Any finance agency can furnish one with convincing proof that use of alcoholic beverages by the ordinary citizen is a definite financial hazard. Headquarters of relief agencies everywhere are full of stories that bear out the contention, "Old rags and bottles" await the junk man at the same place. "For the drunkard and the glutton shall come to poverty" (Prov. 23:21 ASV). Winebibbers and riotous eaters of the flesh are thus warned by the wise man of old against the final effects of strong drink. While the rich and the poor provide most alcoholics, an increasing proportion of those whom society must support because of the use of alcoholic beverages comes from the ranks of the middle class of society—laborers, artisans, and white collar workers. All citizens should be warned, for they can go the way of the alcoholic and drop from affluence to dire need in only a few years.

In Scott County, Tennessee, some years ago there lived a well-to-do farmer. He had a comfortable home, fine stock, good credit, and a high rating as a citizen. Unfortunately he let himself be deceived by the lure of social drinking, feeling sure that a man of his position and business acumen would never become a toper. But twenty years later he was a broken, ruined man whose mind was "a bit tetched" at times. One of the pranks he loved to play at such times was to ask some friend or stranger, especially a physician, "See if you can see anything down my throat." When the person had looked and replied, "Nothing out of the ordinary," the poor fellow would then say with a smirk, "Well, you ought to see something, for I swallowed a good farm, some fine teams, plenty of good cattle, and a good bank account." There he was, a liability to society, whereas, before liquor enslaved him, he was an affluent citizen, paying substantial taxes, and adding a goodly sum annually to the county's income.

During the late summer and autumn of 1914 there were tens of thousands of people in Louisville, Kentucky, in the soup lines. Green Street became so notorious because of vice conditions that its name was changed during World War I. Students from the Baptist and Presbyterian seminaries were finally asked by the welfare workers to aid in making investigations to determine the actual cases needing relief. During one afternoon the author and his teammate visited some thirty-five homes, most of them one and two-room holes in cheap tenement houses. Everywhere they found stark poverty, rags, undernourished children, haggard if not inebriated women. The husband and father, if he remained with his family, in nearly every case was away somewhere, either in jail because of drunken revelries, or in a saloon pandering for a drink.

Since that day, the author has made a study of many cases of poverty, and discovered that more than half of them have been due to the effects of alcoholic drinks. It costs society much more to maintain the impoverished citizens whom drink ruins and their families than all the taxes the liquor industry pays. But the supreme tragedy lies in the fact that rarely will one find such a victim of drink's curse who is not a radical socialist in politics, hating the rich, and ready at any moment to follow the revolutionists who advocate the seizure of property and the establishment of a socialistic state. History proves that freedom dies where poverty reigns; that poverty increases where alcoholic beverages may be secured without restraint by any citizen, for alcoholics sell houses and lands in order to secure their liquor; and that democracy survives only when the causes of poverty are eradicated and people are put in homes which they own.

2. *A Dominant Hope*

If one wishes to see places from which hope is gone and where the future offers little challenge to childhood and youth, let him go to homes where drunkards live. For one thing, the chief aspiration of the alcoholic parent or parents is to secure enough money from some source with which to quench for the moment the accursed desire for alcohol. Secondly, what is left to kindle hope in the mind of a child whose father gets on periodic sprees and comes home to a hungry family with his purse empty? What hope is stirred when instead of affection and encouragement a child has only fear of and contempt for them who begat him and brought him into the world? The author has in his files a letter from a sixteen-year-old girl in which she made a confession after this fashion: "What chance is there, when my dad sneers at me every time I start toward the church, and when he does all he can while in his cups to get me to join him in his drinking? Sometimes I get near the place where I want to slip the bridle and drown it all in his liquor, only I know when I sober up, I'll be a scarlet woman." When enough citizens of a nation are reared by such parents, aspirations among them will almost vanish, and they will be ready to follow the revolutionist who tells them, "It could not be worse; follow me and there is a chance for something better." Such propaganda is readily believed and gathers followers who will bring the woes upon the rich about which James wrote in such a graphic way (James 5: 1–6).

3. *Unswerving Loyalty*

> Land of my sires! What mortal hand
> Can e'er untie the filial band,
> That knits me to thy rugged strand!

Scott included this question in the "Lay of the Last Minstrel." In the same poem are the immortal words which have been quoted by thousands of speakers at patriotic celebrations:

> Breathes there the man, with soul so dead,
> Who never to himself hath said,
> This is my own, my native land!

What encouragement to be patriotic has the poor victim of a perverted appetite when his all has been taken by the vendors of alcoholic beverages? What is there about a government to command the loyalty of the offspring of citizens whose property has been taken by a business which is licensed and protected by their government? What claim to loyalty is given by a state that sends one citizen to the penitentiary for stealing a pig and lets others bask in riches while they through catering to human weaknesses rob men of their homes and incomes and turn them loose as mendicants for others to support?

There are today in the United States several million children who are growing up in homes where alcoholic beverages are set before them, and where the revelings of parents and guests tend to blind youthful eyes to the truth about drinking and to induce young people to ignore all they may have learned in school and at church about the danger of imbibing alcohol in any quantity.

Many such children become the most bitter enemies of the liquor traffic; many others, born with weakened resistance to the lure of narcotics, go the way of the flesh.

4. Cases in Court

A young pastor visited a home where a prospective Sunday school pupil lived. When he turned into the yard he noticed a junior girl playing near the side of the small house. Calling her to him, he asked her name and found that she was the child he was seeking. After a few words with her, he asked if the mother was at home, whereupon the little face showed alarm, the eyes filled with tears, and she suddenly cried, pointing, "She's back there on the porch. But I wouldn't go, preacher, for she's as drunk as an owl." The last three words fairly hissed from the little mouth and the face set with an expression of grim hatred. The pastor did go, however, and found a drunken woman with a partly emptied bottle of gin on a table beside her—a woman whose maudlin mien filled him with utter disgust and caused his soul to cry for someone to avenge the innocent child against the distillers and saloon keepers.

The pastor next visited a home where the husband and father, a short time before, had been seized with a violent attack of delirium tremens shortly after he had reached home from a distillery where he worked. The wild man had tried to kill his baby boy of a few months, but the wife fortunately evaded him and rushed with the child into the street, screaming for help. Neighbors rescued them. The poor victim came near death's door, but faithful and continuous ministration by the pastor, neighbors, and a physician kept him alive, and sanity finally returned. The business that made him a wreck discharged him, but Christians were neighbors to him who had fallen among such men. He was converted, united with a church, found honorable employment, and finally had his household restored. But the pastor's spirit was further enraged against the liquor industry when one day the wife and mother said to him, "God only knows what it means to have to live through such an experience as we knew when he used to get drunk." And then he was made to fear when, with fierce mother anger burning in her soul and flashing like fire from her deep brown eyes, she cried, "How I hate a government that lets cruel, heartless men and women make the stuff and seduce husbands into drinking it!"

5. *A Poet's Warning*

It is high time all Americans who love their country and cherish its traditions of freedom should hear the words of Oliver Goldsmith, for they sound a warning based upon a sociological truth which all human history supports:

> Ill fares the land, to hast'ning ills a prey,
> Where wealth accumulates, and men decay;
> Princes and lords may flourish or may fade;
> A breath can make them, as a breath has made;
> But a bold peasantry, their country's pride,
> When once destroy'd, can ne'er be supplied.

If alcohol struck only the upper social stratum its ravages would not seriously threaten a nation for these people produce only a small fraction of future citizens. But it never stops there. For every drinker among the socially elite, there are ten among the so-called masses, and the proportion will increase unless alcohol is put into irons. Abraham Lincoln declared, "I believe this government

cannot endure permanently half slave and half free."
Were the beloved Emancipator living today and could
see the slavery which alcohol is fastening upon the common people from whom he sprang, he would cry with
equal passion and force, "I know that government cannot
endure long when half its citizenry are being enslaved by
one industry!"

The climax will be reached when a great financial re-
cession comes which throws millions of the common people out of work. With their perverted appetites to be
satisfied, regardless of who may suffer, and their ener-
vated wills and frustrated hearts inflamed, there will be
a hideous mob whose anger cannot be imagined and
whose wild fanaticism will pass beyond the control even
of the adventurers who set them going. If the Tzarist
group, the church lords, and other aristocrats of old Rus-
sia could cry from their graves, they would sound a warning which would arouse the thoughtless who, for the sake
of the tax funds paid by the liquor industry, have closed
their ears against the warnings of history, hardened their
hearts against the appeals of prophets of the day who,
like Jeremiah of old, foretell the doom of a society that
ignores the rights of the masses and refuses to recognize
its responsibility to care for all the people, especially the
weak and least capable members.

II. MENACING MANHOOD

It is now time for patriots everywhere to be reminded
of other words from Abraham Lincoln, for there is a dangerous trend away from the basic idea of democracy. It
is the citizen for whom the state exists; the state must,
therefore, exalt, protect, and develop the citizen regardless of his degree of culture. The words of the Emancipa-

tor are: . . . "this nation, under God, shall have a new birth of freedom; and that government of the people, by the people, and for the people, shall not perish from the earth." How is this ideal being threatened?

1. *By Handicapped Citizens*

"Preacher, will you go to the general sessions court this week and see if you can persuade the judge to restore my driver's license?" The request was made during the week while this chapter was being finished. The father of five children, the youngest a baby of four weeks, had been caught by a traffic officer before he in his partially intoxicated condition caused a highway accident. He had sobered up; his fellow churchmen had taken him in hand; he had come to the altar in a truly repentant frame of mind; he had vowed "Never again." Without the driver's license he would lose his job or else spend one third of his pay for taxi service. The same week in the same community a woman was persuaded to try again, after she had packed her clothes and was ready to sue a drinking husband for divorce.

The two mentioned in the preceding paragraph are representative of millions of people in the nation who are being menaced by alcohol, and whose innocent companions and offspring are being made to suffer. A visit to the laborer's home revealed the usual condition of squalor and aroused again the bitter resentment of heart against a government that will allow innocent little ones to suffer and a mother to live under the shadow of fear and in the midst of want, just because thoughtless or deceived citizens, for the sake of easy gain, pander to such as he whose weaknesses make him helpless against those who deal in intoxicants.

2. What About the Future?

"Whatsoever a man soweth, that shall he also reap" (Gal. 6 : 7). Science has discovered too much about what alcohol in the human body does to handicap one's off-spring for anyone ever to be deceived by propaganda paid for by money received from the sale of the product which, when it affects the lives of a large enough proportion of the future population, will bring destruction to the nation.

Dr. Rodolfo Demme of Berne, Switzerland, a noted pediatrician, made some accurate checks. He selected ten families in which the father, and in some cases the mother, were alcoholics. Ten families of total abstainers were selected, families of the same background as the others. The offspring of these were as follows: *Alcoholics:* 57 children, of whom 12 died in infancy, 12 were defective physically, 8 were mentally retarded, 5 became alcoholics, and only 9 became normal men and women. *Abstainers:* 61 children, of whom 5 died in infancy, 2 had physical defects, 2 were mentally defective, none became an alcoholic, and 50 were normal adults.

III. Burdening Good Backs

1. Increasing Tax Load

One of the spurious claims of the friends of beverage alcohol is that tax revenue brought in by the legalization of the business reduces the tax burden elsewhere. The Federal Bureau of Investigation can furnish the figures to show the enormous cost to society for the apprehension, conviction, and support of criminals, many of whom have been produced through the use of alcoholic beverages; the mounting cost of hospitalization for all kinds of alcoholics and for wounded and maimed people whom drink produces in an ever-increasing number; maintenance of the increasing number of traffic and general police officers due to the consumption of alcoholic beverages.

The 1949 census of manufacturers in the United States showed that for every million dollars spent for beer, 62 people were given employment; the same sum spent for soft drinks gave employment to 106, and for lumber 135. With modern methods of brewing, bottling, packaging, and shipping, the ratio of employees to income drops down. The production of alcohol by synthetic methods will both reduce the number of employees needed in the production of distilled spirits and eliminate entirely the need for grains.

The argument of financial gain to a state that allows the manufacture and sale of intoxicants falls to pieces before cold facts!

2. *Declining Safety Margin*

There is little need to present data in support of the contention that the mania for speed is left uncontrolled when alcohol takes over the human brain. Even with only .07 per cent of alcohol in the blood stream, the reflex centers of the brain are so affected that a drinking driver runs five times the risk of causing an accident as the sober driver does. Pedestrians who drink are also in far graver danger of meeting accident and death than are sober people. Of 2,472 walkers killed in traffic in New York City, more than one fourth had above .01 per cent of alcohol in their blood. The reckless driver and the careless pedestrian are both offspring of alcoholic beverages; one is cocksure that he can drive more carefully than ever, the other ignores all safety zones!

The imagination is staggered by the rapid increase in the production of mechanical marvels. Every one of these becomes a bit more complex and a bit faster in operation. In olden times the drunk could turn his horse loose toward home and, with rare exceptions, the beast returned without attention from the occupant of the vehicle behind him. But with the advent of the automobile, such safety was gone. When the cars of 1915 happened to collide, the speed was so low that fatalities were rare. But with speeds up to 100 miles per hour, the results inevitably are tragic. On the old-fashioned steam engine the governor balls, operated by centrifugal force, controlled the speed of the engine; it is not so with the modern automobile. On the contrary, the alcohol in one's blood removes the governor within, the foot presses the accelerator more heavily, and disaster results. With the advent of jet propelled machinery and the near advent of atomic (perhaps hydrogen) powered machinery, the speed passes comprehension, and every mile added to speed increases the danger from any narcotic that slows the brain reflexes and stunts the will.

3. *Our Complex Society*

Even as machinery becomes more complicated and demands more efficient management, so does the social, industrial, financial, and political world grow more complex. The Pentagon Building in Alexandria, Virginia, across from Washington, is a symbol of the vast complexity that bureaucracy has imposed upon the nation. In turn, the complexity of national organization acts as a pattern for all political as well as other units below it.

What chance has an alcoholic to do otherwise than wreck the machinery of a banking chain, an industrial enterprise, or some department of state? Reason should compel all citizens to realize that split-second decisions and even moderate amounts of alcohol in the blood can never go together.

4. *Death or Else*

A driver was passing in front of Belmont College in Nashville, Tennessee. He had turned the corner of Sixteenth Avenue, South, to the right when behind a car a few feet in front of him a little girl of some seven years dashed into the street, not ten feet beyond the front bumper of his car. Almost instantaneous was the reflex that removed a foot from the accelerator and slammed it on the brakes. The car stopped just as the child's skirt brushed the end of the bumper. Had there been alcohol in that driver's brain, the child would have been injured, perhaps the life crushed out of her, for the difference between sparing a life and killing a pedestrian is often the difference between the split-second reflexive action of a sober driver and the momentary delay in the reflexes caused by alcohol. The shadows of death were kept from a Nashville home because, among other things, a citizen was wise enough never to touch alcoholic beverages. The threat of a social cataclysm in our nation can greatly be removed if the nation compels all citizens to be sober.

The dulling effect of alcohol upon the entire nervous system is too evident for anyone to be deceived by the subtle propaganda of the liquor industry. With the rapid modern machinery and the growing speed and complexity of traffic, one no longer is allowed minutes to make decisions and to act upon them; he has only split seconds! Whosoever, therefore, would save himself from the grim probability of snuffing out the life of an innocent pedestrian, or maybe the lives of a carload of helpless people, will never allow the lure of removing any inhibitions or restraints upon his spirit to lead him to indulge even in the mildest of alcoholic beverages.

SUGGESTED TOPICS FOR DISCUSSION

1. Secure from the traffic court a list of accidents in your city or county for the past month and check to see what proportion of them involved drivers who had been drinking.
2. Check the divorce list for the year and find out how many were due to drinking.
3. See if you can find out what proportion of the needy of your county or city have been brought to poverty by the use of alcohol.
4. When is it safe to drink? And where?

I. DANGER LIES IN MISUSE

    1. Lessons from the Sabbath

    2. Lessons from Sacrifices

    3. Food and Drink

    4. Revelation Clear Enough

II. ALCOHOLIC BEVERAGES CONDEMNED

    1. Primitive Man Not Blinded

    2. A Will-o'-the Wisp

    3. Alcoholics Described and Admonished

III. PASSAGES THAT PUZZLE

    1. The Miracle at Cana

    2. The Memorial Supper

6

ALCOHOL IN THE BIBLE

SUPPORT can be found in the Bible for any assumption or claim, if texts are selected without regard to the total teaching of the Book on the matter. Today, as during the centuries since Christianity had its beginning in Galilee and Judea, people who wish to make excuses for indulgence in any questionable practice do not hesitate to quote the Bible when defending themselves or their business. All students should, therefore, be on guard against such hypocritical use of the Word of God as is often made by those connected with the trade in alcoholic beverages. A careful study of the entire Bible, not a few isolated passages from it, will show what it teaches regarding the matter.

I. DANGER LIES IN MISUSE

1. *Lessons from the Sabbath*

"The sabbath was made for man, and not man for the sabbath" (Mark 2:27). With that terse statement Jesus revealed an entire field of fact which mankind too often ignores. One may well paraphrase the statement thus: "Everything the Creator put here can be used for man's good; see to it that you do not pervert its use and make that which was intended to do good into a means of harm or slavery." In applying this fundamental principle of conduct, civilized society must compel its members to refrain from the misuse of everything that may prove to be a bane.

There is lack of wisdom when a nation places strict prohibitions against the misuse of opiates and refuses to safeguard the public against the misuse of narcotics. What wisdom is there in a law that controls the highways, but allows vendors of alcoholic beverages to put in jeopardy every good citizen who uses the roads? The highways were made for man, for all citizens; would not wisdom impel a wise state to see to it that the vast majority of people are protected against a business that is responsible for drinking drivers, hence for wreckage and death on the highways? Rigid laws control travel on trains and planes, the use of the water power, electricity, and so on. Prohibition laws had their origin from God—eight of the Ten Commandments are prohibition laws—"Thou shalt not." Like the sabbath of the days when Jesus was on earth, used by priests to enslave their fellows, alcohol is used today to enslave the masses that makers and vendors may fatten their purses and enjoy luxurious living.

2. Lessons from Sacrifices

Because of man's instinctive knowledge about God; because of the innate tendency of uncultured man to make the deity tangible through images; because of the struggle of leaders to reach toward the ideal state which man's spirit knows must exist somewhere, sometime; and because the outreach of the soul for God can never be eradicated from the human family, worship will continue. Religion cannot be destroyed. But the holy impulses which drive man to the practice of religion can also enslave him. This is proved by the manner in which the Mikado of Japan was worshiped by his subjects before World War II. The danger is attested by the reaction of the lay world in the presence of an honored minister of the gospel, especially when that minister wears distinctive clerical dress. It may be studied by examining the slow but steady decline in individual worship such as Abraham, Jacob, and others practiced, and the rise of a powerful priestly class in Israel with Jerusalem as the holy city.

God through Isaiah and other prophets denounced the perverted sacrificial system. "Bring no more vain oblations; incense is an abomination unto me; the new moons and sabbaths, the calling of assemblies, I cannot away with; it is iniquity, even the solemn meeting. Your new moons and your appointed feasts my soul hateth: they are a trouble unto me; I am weary to bear [put up with] them" (Isa. 1:13–14). Hosea foretold the day when the system of sacrifices would cease (Hos. 2:11). John the Baptist castigated the hypocritical people of his day who had been so enslaved by the mechanics of their religion that they had lost sight of its moral and spiritual nature. Make evident a repentant heart, then come and ask me to baptize you, is the challenge he gave them (Luke 3:8). Worship had so degenerated and the sacrificial system been so degraded when Jesus was here that the Master of men in righteous indignation and holy zeal drove the grafting priests and their helpers from the temple area as he would have driven out wild beasts (John 2:15).

God made no mistake, however, when he established the system of worship which Moses devised for the Hebrews. Let God's called men serve as he intended them to do, and all other people will be blessed through them and man's welfare will be promoted thereby. When God's altars represent real sacrifices that grow out of a spirit of self-abnegation and desire to serve, they always bless individuals and raise society to higher planes. Likewise, when everything else, including alcohol, is kept where the Creator intended it to be used, man is always benefited thereby.

3. Food and Drink

The Bible has much to say about food and many wise words about drink. Throughout the Book gluttony is denounced and winebibbing decried. "Be not among winebibbers; among riotous eaters of flesh: for the drunkard and the glutton shall come to poverty" (Prov. 23:20–21). The death penalty was put upon the chronic gluttonous alcoholic (Deut. 21:20). "Put a knife to thy throat, if thou be a man given to appetite," is the advice of Solomon (Prov. 23:2 asv). Peter warned against the excesses of the people of olden times (1 Peter 4:3). Joel railed against the drunkards of his day, telling them that the enemy would invade their land and destroy the source of their wine (Joel 1:5).

God provides even the unregenerate with food and drink and raiment (Deut. 10:18). Solomon, who had access to all kinds of rich foods and costly wines, prayed, "Feed me with the food that is needful for me" (Prov. 30:8 asv). Food was provided in Eden from trees (Gen. 2:9) and not from fermentation vats. Noah was instructed to store the ark with "all food that is eaten" (Gen. 6:21). The Hebrews were given specific instructions about providing food after they had entered Canaan (Lev. 19:23, 25). Evidence of real faith is found in giving raiment to the naked and food to the hungry (James 2:15–16). When Lemuel's mother warned him against drinking wine, she pointed out that only they who were ready to perish (to be cast out) and they who were deeply depressed should be given wine (Prov. 31: 1–7). A good physician can readily explain how this advice was a medical prescription; it was never intended to give people any basis upon which to defend the traffic in alcoholic beverages.

4. Revelation Clear Enough

While the use of wine as a beverage is referred to many times in the Bible, the honest scholar and student will not overlook some pertinent facts about it: Science had not uncovered the real nature of alcohol. If God had impelled his prophets to condemn it in the light of facts well known today, no one would have been able to interpret their words; for them the world would still have been flat. The narcotic and anesthetic nature of alcohol was unknown.

The Bible repeatedly and with stern dogmatism condemns wine. The winepress is a metaphor, associated with the wrath of God (Rev. 19:15). Wine is a figure of terrible anger and is listed among the things which voluptuous, wicked Babylon enjoyed and then lost (Rev. 14:8–10; 16:19). It is associated with gross adultery (Rev. 17:2) and with hell fire (Rev. 14:10). Elderly women are warned against the use of too much wine (Titus 2:3)—were some of them alcoholics? Paul commanded men to refrain from wine and to seek rather to be filled with the Spirit of God (Eph. 5:18). Elders, ministers, and priests—all who act as spiritual leaders —are commanded to be teetotalers (1 Tim. 3:2). Numerous other references may be given to show that alcoholic beverages are never in God's Word classed as food or as essential to man's diet.

II. ALCOHOLIC BEVERAGES CONDEMNED

1. *Primitive Man Not Blinded*

In spite of the ignorance of mankind, when judged by modern standards of learning, enough was known about health and moral well-being for all to be warned about the evils of intemperance, both in eating and in the use of alcoholic beverages. But, as is true today so it was in the ages past, they who indulged always made an excuse for their sin. Whether the priest at the altar or the prince in the palace, when strong drink once has fastened its narcotic hold upon the nervous system, its victim not only does not want to quit drinking but is usually the strongest defender of the thing that enslaves him. Numerous records from the past show that primitive man recognized the danger in wine and other fermented drinks. Mohammed banned alcoholic beverages from all the altars and worshipers of Allah!

2. *A Will-o'-the-Wisp*

The writer of Proverbs impersonates wine as a grinning ogre, leading her victims into various forms of trouble and disaster only to watch them suffer and to deride them for their folly in allowing themselves to be seduced by her. "Wine is a mocker" (Prov. 20:1) literally means, "Wine at last laughs to scorn them who have been deceived by her."

To realize the full meaning of the word painting, take a look at the victim of man's lust for sex pleasure. A news item tells the story of an attractive young woman whose "boy friend" had spurned her request to be married to him. They had a quarrel about it, he is reported as telling the police, so he left his bachelor apartment for some time. When he returned he found that she had committed suicide, so he crammed her body in a bag, drove with it to a bridge, and dumped it into the Hudson River. That was the gist of the tragic story. What it did not tell was the despair of the girl when she realized that she had paid a terrible price for the few hours of excitement which the man had provided for her in return for her honor and her virtue. Even so, the alcoholic can tell how much he has lost in return for drink, and often he, like that poor girl, destroys his own life rather than face the consequences of his self-imposed slavery.

3. Alcoholics Described and Admonished

The Bible describes in a graphic manner the state of the victim of alcohol. "Who hath woe? Who hath sorrow? . . . Who hath wounds without cause? Who hath redness of eyes?" This dramatic inquiry should challenge all to profit from the answer: "They that tarry long at the wine; they that go to seek out mixed wine" (Prov. 23:29–30 ASV). Then follows the admonition of the man whom God characterized as the wisest man who had lived or ever should live on earth: "Look not thou upon the wine when it is red, when it sparkleth in the cup, when it goeth down smoothly" (Prov. 23:31 ASV).

A careful study of drunkenness, or alcoholism, made in the light of present-day knowledge about strong drink, will lead one to see a sixfold reason for Solomon's admonition: Alcohol is a narcotic and anesthetic, hence is a dangerous drug. Alcohol attacks the brain and causes its victim to imagine vain things, to see strange visions.

Civil courts reveal the extent to which strong drink provides the grist for the divorce mills because it often leads its victims to babble. The surest ally of enemy spies in any land is the tongue which alcohol has loosened and left unguarded. Alcohol tampers with the balance wheel of the body which reels and wobbles and is obsessed by hallucinations about time and place. Alcohol brings to its victims brawls with their consequent "wounds without cause," wounds often unfelt until the drunken debauch has passed. Alcohol creates a slavish desire for itself, and every drink the victim takes binds more securely about his body and mind and soul the chains of slavery. This sixfold condemnation of alcoholic beverages is found in Proverbs 23:30-35. If it holds against the use of wine, the only intoxicant known in Solomon's palace, how much more serious would it be if he were to write it against distilled spirits?

The account of Belshazzar's feast becomes all the more gruesome when the conditions that made the tragic close of it possible are known. The wine-befuddled king was stricken with horror by the mysterious handwriting on the wall of the palace banquet room. Without the city the Persians were preparing for the coup that overthrew Babylon. Daniel was brought in and interpreted the strange vision which the king had seen. The extent of the drunkenness of Belshazzar is revealed by the fact that, in spite of the calamity which Daniel foretold, the king rewarded him richly.

Meanwhile, Cyrus and his Persians, aided by his uncle, Darius the Mede, were diverting the waters of the Euphrates River. At the strategic hour when the king and his courtiers were drunk, the enemy went under the walls of the city along the emptied stream bed, and disaster resulted. This did not come about because of the superior ability of the Persian soldiers, for they had sought in vain for two years to conquer the city. The tragedy is another of the shameful defeats which nations have suffered because rulers have loved wine more than wisdom, the momentary exuberance of intoxication more than the prolonged acclaim of mankind. God's Word provides little comfort for them who are engaged in promoting or protecting the traffic in alcoholic beverages. It holds no brief for any person who wishes to have an alibi for being a user of them.

III. PASSAGES THAT PUZZLE

There are many references in the Bible to wine and other intoxicants. Some of these, like Paul's advice to Timothy about using wine for his stomach's sake (discussed in chapter 1 of this book), are used readily by supporters of the traffic in alcoholic beverages as well as by many who want an alibi for their own drinking. Other outstanding passages of this kind are discussed briefly.

1. *The Miracle at Cana*

"Jesus turned the water into wine at Cana of Galilee" has many times been said by a defender of the use of alcoholic beverages. The failure of the friends of temperance to demand proof that Jesus made an intoxicating drink has been harmful. People have gone on taking it for granted that it was intoxicating wine. Do the facts sustain that view?

The Greek word used in the passage for wine is *oinos,* and it did not always refer to a fermented drink. Throughout ancient times the word was used to refer to fruit juices, primarily grape juice, without regard to whether or not it was fermented, or had even turned to vinegar. Recipes for preparing various kinds of wines without fermentation have been preserved by writers of antiquity; and the common practice of boiling their wines, and also of largely diluting them, showed that the action of fermentation was not regarded by the ancients as essential to the existence of *oinos*. Many authorities agree that the Greek use of *oinos* included fresh grape juice.

The Greek text of the New Testament has *oinos* in Mark 15:23, but in Matthew the word for vinegar appears. The drink, administered as a sedative, had lost its alcoholic content but still was *oinos!* Throughout the Septuagint (early Greek translation of the Old Testament), *oinos* was used to translate both *yayin* or fermented juice and *tirosh* or fresh juice. So to claim that *oinos* always referred in the New Testament to an alcoholic beverage is to ignore facts.

Now look at the use of the word in John 2:1–11. It should be kept in mind that the miracles of Jesus always had a beneficent motive behind them; he did not do mighty works to be seen of men. The author believes that Jesus, in changing the water into *oinos*, chose to create fresh grape juice instead of fermented wine. In other words, in making the wine, the natural thing for the Master to do, and the direct thing, was to create fresh grape juice. "But how could that fool the ruler of the feast?" one will ask. It is not merely indulging in wishful thinking when one declares that, being made by the Creator, the new juice contained the full richness and sweetness of the juice which was drunk by Adam and Eve in Eden; hence the ruler of the feast was surprised. Furthermore, what could have been more delightful to guests already somewhat surfeited with alcohol than the rich, luscious, soothing juice fresh from the hands of the Lord?

Even those who believe that the wine which Jesus made from the water at Cana was fermented wine must reckon with the fact that this miracle does not condone the drinking of alcoholic beverages in our day. Pure water was then very scarce. There was also the problem of preservation of the pure grape juice which fermentation took care of. This miracle can never be logically advanced as an argument for the liquor traffic.

2. *The Memorial Supper*

Much has been made of the use of wine in connection with the institution of the Memorial Supper. But by what authority had anyone ever claimed that Jesus used fermented wine on that occasion? To answer that question, take a look at the Passover and the rules which surrounded it.

Wine is not mentioned in passages telling about the institution of the Passover. Only the roast lamb, the bitter herbs or salad, and the unleavened bread were prescribed by the Lord (Exodus 12). First references to the meal make no mention of wine. "Liquors" in Exodus 22 : 29 in the Authorized Version is rendered in the American Standard Version thus, "Thou shalt not delay to offer of thy harvest, and of the outflow of thy presses." According to a noted Hebrew scholar, Fuerst, the word translated "liquors" could have referred only to fresh fruit juice. Nazirites could not be debarred from the

Passover; they were represented in many homes; they could not drink fermented juices; so it is certain that such were not served during the meal.

When the Passover was eaten before Sinai, wine was not used (Num. 9:9-14). The first observance of it in Canaan makes no mention of wine (Josh. 5:10-12). When Moses renewed the regulations surrounding the meal he made no mention of wine (Deut. 16:2-6). Until the time of Christ the meal was often referred to as the feast of unleavened bread (Ex. 12:17; Deut. 16:16).

It is quite evident, therefore, that the Jewish lawyers, probably influenced by pagan sources, came to feel that the Passover was incomplete without the libations in wine, so the Talmudic law which prescribed wine superseded the Mosaic law in many places of sacrifice. However, the custom of using wine made from fresh-pressed grapes, or pressed from raisins soaked overnight for the purpose, prevails among orthodox Jews until today. "The prohibition against the presence of ferment and the use of all fermented articles was explicit and emphatic." The Jewish encyclopedia makes it quite clear that originally the Passover did not include fermented wine. It says, "The phrase 'to eat' in the prohibition was construed to include any use of leaven as nourishment (by drinking, for instance). In fact, neither advantage nor enjoyment might be drawn from leaven during the festival." Gesenius, a noted Hebrew scholar, declares that the prohibition, "No leaven found in your houses" (Ex. 12:19 ASV) referred to wine as well as bread. "Their drink during the time of the feast," he says, "is either pure water or raisin wine prepared by themselves, but no kind of leaven must be added."

Nowhere in the accounts of the Lord's Supper is wine

found. "He took the cup" (Matt. 26:27) refers to the cup just used during the Passover where no ferment was allowed, not even in the house where the supper was prepared (Ex. 12:15). When Jesus spoke of the content of the cup he called it the fruit of the vine (Matt. 26:29). Mark gives the same report of the occasion (Mark 14:22-25), and Luke's version is quite similar (Luke 22:14-20). One is backed by good witnesses when he declares that in instituting the Memorial Supper the Lord did not use intoxicating wine; he used the natural "blood of the grape" for it was to symbolize for future ages the blood he shed as the Paschal Lamb (John 1:29, 36).

SUGGESTED TOPICS FOR DISCUSSION

1. Show how the American slave owner once used the Bible to defend his right to possess slaves.
2. Discuss the difference between prohibition of the sale of opiates and, if there be such in your city, prohibition of the sale of alcoholic beverages.
3. Make a list of all Bible passages that condemn the uncontrolled use of alcoholic beverages and, over against this list, put the Scriptures that definitely approve such.
4. Seek for information that shows the attitude of various modern rulers toward strong drink, also that of leading churchmen toward it.

CHAPTER 7 OUTLINE

I. ANCIENT REFORMERS STERN
   1. In Oriental Countries
   2. Southern Asia and Control
   3. Liquor Confounds Southern Europe
   4. Mighty Greece Falls

II. THE WESTERN WORLD AND WINE
   1. Britain Harmed by Drink
   2. The Public Aroused

III. BATTLING IN THE UNITED STATES
   1. Marked Men
   2. A Mighty Warrior Appears

IV. THE NOBLE EXPERIMENT
   1. During Revolutionary Days
   2. Rising Religious Opposition
   3. Pre-Civil War Days
   4. Reaching the Climax

7

EFFORTS AT CONTROL

A FALLACY that has done great harm in the efforts to control alcohol is that prohibition was a failure because it did not prohibit. What the enemies of statutory control of beverage alcohol really imply by the statement is that prohibition was a failure because it did not absolutely destroy the traffic. Such an argument is never used to prove the failure of other statutes. For example, one never hears a friend of liquor advocate repeal of the laws against theft because they do not obliterate thieves. Yet the effort to eliminate theft has been costing society many times as much as the infrequent efforts to control beverage alcohol. One never hears a social drinker arguing for the repeal of laws governing the sale of opiates because dope peddlers have never been entirely removed from under cover. "Thou shalt not kill" is a part of the moral code of the ages; man has not enforced it absolutely. Yet neither God nor civilized society has ever repealed the law. Proper evaluation of the worth of any effort at control should, therefore, be based upon what it does to reduce the consumption of alcoholic beverages and thus to relieve society of the baneful effects which the traffic places upon the nation that tolerates it and upon the people who use it and their families. Wisdom will never allow her child to be content with what is; he must see what may be because of what is.

I. ANCIENT REFORMERS STERN

1. *In Oriental Countries*

More than twelve hundred years before Christ the evils of alcohol had been recognized by statesmen in China. The nation that produced pulp paper, gunpowder, and other useful things long before the Anglo-Saxon race came into being degenerated because of drink and by 1100 B.C. had turned itself into a nation of paupers who were ruled by heartless pampered lords. So deplorable were conditions that a good emperor who arose at that time issued an edict entitled "Announcement About Drunkenness." In the preamble to the document are these words, "Our people have been greatly disorganized, and lost their virtue, which can be traced to their indulgence in spirits." The edict cited the destruction of the previous dynasty, that of Yin, against whom "heaven sent down ruin and showed no love for Yin, because of such excesses." So the successor to the Yin dynasty set up prohibition laws to correct many of the evils which had ruined the former ruling family.

The edict imposed the death penalty upon social drinkers. Officers were to apprehend any company of drinkers and "send them to Chow, where I will put them to death." One can readily imagine how quickly the traffic in such beverages was curtailed. History for the next five hundred years shows to what extent China was blessed by the prohibition movement, for developments during that era could never have been designed nor carried out by any but a sober people. But the control was gradually relaxed; the use of wine was added to the native ales; priests became more drunken and debauched, and the curse of strong drink re-entered palace walls. By 275 B.C. conditions were so bad that Mencius issued strong denunciations against the venal priesthood for their excessive use of wine and warned all other citizens against the curse of intoxicants.

2. Southern Asia and Control

Next to the civilization of China, if not older than it, is that of India, Persia, and the Euphrates Valley. From the meager records which the ancient peoples left for us, we find repeated evidences of the struggle to eliminate the drink habit through control of the makers and vendors of alcoholic beverages. One favorite intoxicating drink required the use of milk, and its makers advanced one of the stock arguments of modern brewers and distillers, namely: "Thine intoxication is that which giveth abundance of cows." The modern brewer tells of increased grain production due to beer making.

Conditions finally became so distressing that a social revolution rose against the alcohol industry and under Manu the great lawgiver, rigid prohibitions were issued against the business. Conditions in India improved and a stronger government arose. But before a generation had arisen whose parentage was sober, the East India Company from Great Britain entered the country and soon not only wine but distilled spirits were being dispensed to the ignorant peoples. For permitting this and other sins against a helpless land, England has at last suffered the loss of all her Indian possessions. Had she sent mission workers instead of beer barrels and cases of Scotch, India would today be a Christian nation and another rich crown colony in the British Empire.

Persia trained her children during the first centuries

of her growing might to be total abstainers. Rigid controls were held over the production of wine and brews. Even as late as the reign of Cyrus the Great, little intoxication could be found in the nation. Cyrus, a temperate man, lived to a ripe old age. The historian Xenophon says that the use of wine at altars was carefully controlled and restricted to small amounts at any service.

3. *Liquor Confounds Southern Europe*

No section of the world has been more completely under the control of the liquor industry for the past five hundred years than Europe. The wine makers of France exert a powerful influence over the government of that country. This is one reason why a recent premier of France who sought to substitute milk for wine in the diet of children was soon ousted from his office. The fruit of the vine, one of nature's choicest and richest foods, has thus for ages been made a curse to European countries and has retarded the development of peoples who have in their nature the spark of creative artistry.

Pliny, the renowned early historian, tells us that the ancient priests of Rome used a libation of milk when they worshiped at the pagan altars. For some centuries after Rome was founded the vice of drunkenness was practically unknown. The period of the republic was the result of this prohibition era which allowed time and opportunity for the rise of creative geniuses and for the conquests by military strategists who made Rome mistress of the world. One prohibition law of the era forbade any woman to drink wine. It also prohibited the use of wine by males until after they had reached the age of thirty-five years. Romulus looked upon drunkenness as "the grand incentive for lewdness." A woman who became intoxicated was subject to the death penalty. One nobleman killed his wife because she had become drunk without asking his permission to touch the wine, and the court acquitted him of murder.

In 183 B.C. the Roman senate passed a law putting rigid controls upon the worship of Bacchus, the god of wine, whose temples had become dens of indescribable excesses. All the vineyards in Champagne were once destroyed in order to root out the source of wine which had so corrupted the populace. The Roman senate also passed a law during the days of the republic which debarred from his seat any member guilty of public drunkenness. But the wealthy, powerful republic begat corruption among politicians and the gentry. Roman power and the vast empire which it developed and for centuries directed were gradually sapped by the growing indulgence in alcoholic beverages. Gibbon tells us in his *Decline and Fall of the Roman Empire* how the corrupt politicians slowly enslaved the masses whom they pauperized in order to get their votes and so corrupted the senate that it lost the respect of the nation. Then arose the dictatorial emperors and in the end the vast Holy Roman Empire went to pieces before the mighty Reformation movement.

4. *Mighty Greece Falls*

Before the days of Philip II and his dissipated son, Alexander the Great, there had been a period of some five centuries during which the pioneer Hellenic blood and spirit had developed a great republic and when the creative genius of a free race was little handicapped by human vices, hence largely unrestricted in productivity. Strict prohibition laws prevailed. Inspectors of public

morals were appointed by the government with authority to examine people, to punish those guilty of drunkenness, and to reward worthy citizens. The famous Court
of the Areopagus was made up of brilliant lawyers and
renowned orators. It enforced rigid prohibition laws. A
man known to visit taverns and public houses could not
gain a seat. A member who was convicted of immoral
conduct was expelled. Solon, the great lawgiver, made
drunkenness of a member of the court a felony punish-
able by death. He classed taverns with houses of prostitution. In ancient Sparta intemperance in drink was
so despised that parents often would cause a slave to
become intoxicated that they might thus display to their
children how great a fool strong drink makes one become. Plato included rigid prohibition laws in his republic, banning the use of all intoxicants for women and
children and limiting the use by men to those beyond
thirty years of age.

Across the pages of history, from very ancient times to
the present, one may see concrete evidence of the age-
old struggle by wise leaders of the social body to control
the traffic in alcoholic beverages. The prohibition movement is not a modern thing that was thrust upon mankind by puritanical fanatics; it is the natural,
spontaneous uprising of prophetic ministers of religion
and farseeing statesmen, of teachers and philosophers, of
rulers and industrial lords, and of genuine patriots of all
generations. To be associated with any organization that
has for its aim the absolute banishment of the traffic in
beverage alcohol is to be joined to one of the great com-
panies of the ages—Hammurabi and Moses, great law-
givers, Romulus, fabled founder of Rome, Plato, father
of philosophy, besides many great modern souls.

II. THE WESTERN WORLD AND WINE

1. *Britain Harmed by Drink*

Wine has been used for centuries by the people of Europe. Long before Alfred united the various tribes of the British Isles into a kingdom, the Angles and the Saxons, the Picts and the Celts used much wine in all their feasts. Danes from across the channel were likewise great tipplers. Edmund I was slain during a drunken revel in the palace, when one of his lords became angry and the others were too drunk to interfere when the king was attacked. During the lush years under Edward the Confessor the making and use of alcoholic beverages were encouraged and festive occasions degenerated into displays of bestial gluttony and drunken rioting.

The Battle of Hastings, September 28, 1066, was lost by the drunken forces of King Harold, who spent the night before in revelings, to the sober troops of the Duke of Normandy, who spent the night in fasting and prayer. The Normans, however, never came in sufficient numbers to change the character of the people of the British Isles. Gradually they were amalgamated, the lure of wine overcame the spirit of the conquering force, and, instead of helping make a sober nation, they fell victims of the alcoholism that was England's curse.

By the time of the reign of Henry I, degeneracy had taken such hold of the people that the king taught his son to drink and looked with pleasure upon the drunken antics of the young man. But when the son was en route to claim the daughter of the king of France as his bride he took along a goodly supply of wine. Before reaching the port in France he passed it out to seamen and guests alike and a drunken orgy followed during which the tipsy helmsman let the ship crash against a big rock near the shore and all on board were drowned except the ship's butcher who escaped by clinging to an unsubmerged mast of the craft.

Henry II saw the devastation which alcohol was creating and set up laws to control its use. The amount of liquor that could be served during a banquet, as well as the amount of meats, was limited. The laws were strengthened during the reign of Edward III (A.D. 1363). By the end of that century the deplorable conditions described by Chaucer in *The Canterbury Tales* had developed. James I, enticed by revenue, encouraged the making and sale of wines, but before long the conditions created by the liquor industry had become so terrible that he changed his attitude and had laws passed which placed heavy penalties upon drunkards. Charles I also sought to curb the industry but, as is always true, it would not be curbed. England became known as the "Land of Drunkards," and Cromwell and his sober, psalm-singing peasant troops had little trouble defeating the aristocracy, many of whom along with Charles lost their heads. With the downfall of Charles I the landed gentry of the nation suffered huge losses and England's government was changed. Daniel Defoe tells us that the gentry were responsible for the gross immorality which was handed down to the poorer sort, who "still love to be like their betters."

2. *The Public Aroused*

An increasing death rate from alcoholism throughout the British Isles and from accidents and fights caused by drinking, a spreading crime wave, and the mounting cost of providing care for paupers produced by strong drink led to the upsurge of temperance sentiment during the nineteenth century. Medical societies led in such movements. Scientific investigations were made which revealed the inescapable fact that the nation which licenses grog shops will, at great and mounting cost, care for the paupers which alcoholic beverages produce. In 1851, Parliament had come so completely under the control of the liquor forces that all restrictions upon the manufacture and sale of beverages were removed. The argument which proponents of the bill in Parliament made were exactly the same as are presented today, namely: "Unrestricted sales of liquors will make for the comfort of the people and for better health, because it will result in providing better drinks, and the temptation to run disorderly houses will thereby be removed from sellers." Even the renowned Duke of Wellington at first fell for this argument.

Within two weeks after the law went into effect, conditions in some population centers were terrible. During the first year, 24,342 free licenses were granted to sellers. The *London Globe* and other daily newspapers began printing lurid stories about moral conditions and clamoring for restrictions on the trade. Within ten years the aroused populace had made changes under local option rights which they had wrung from Parliament. By 1869, there were more than one thousand parishes in the province of Canterbury in which there was neither a tavern nor a public house nor a beer shop. As a result of the control the following benefits came: Infant mortality dropped; there was little failure to make regular payment of rentals; while wages did not materially increase "the people live better because they spend none of it for ale."

A rector in one province reported, "We have had no case for the police since I came here." The *Edinburgh Review* of January, 1873, reported, "We have seen a bit of 89 estates [American plantations] in England and Scotland where the drink traffic has been suppressed with the very happiest results."

III. BATTLING IN THE UNITED STATES

Every student of reform movements in the United States must be struck by the fact that from early colonial days a fight against beverage alcohol has been going on. W. H. Daniels well says, "Alcohol has been treated as a wolf, on which, from time to time, as his ravages become more awful and cruel, the colony or State has been forced to set the sharp teeth and strong muscles of the law." [1] Back and forth the pendulum has swung. Each time a reform movement has been pressed it has stalled too soon and the friends of beverage alcohol have been able to swing society to the other direction. As we are well into the second half of the twentieth century the pendulum has begun its forward stroke; one may well predict that the rising tide of resentment and publicity against the liquor industry will not easily be stayed.

1. *Marked Men*

The first crusaders for temperance in the nation were marked men. In 1789, a group of farmers in Connecticut banded together to protect themselves against drunken farm hands. They refused to provide beverages for their laborers. Immediately these landlords were boycotted. They were hissed on the streets of Litchfield. The tails of

[1] W. H. Daniels, *The Temperance Reform and Its Great Reformers* (New York: Nelson & Phillips, 1878), p. 6.

their horses were sheared to resemble those of mules. Some had fences broken down. Other indignities were heaped upon them and they were branded as fanatics. In 1897, a Methodist conference in Virginia voted heartily to abandon the use of alcoholic beverages and to induce all others to do the same. In 1808, the Union Temperance Society was organized at Saratoga, New York, with 43 male members. They pledged not to drink intoxicants and to do all they could to get others to cease to drink.

Between 1808, when the first temperance society was organized, and 1826 due trial was made on behalf of temperance, and the friends of sobriety saw that the temperance movement must inevitably fail. As long as beverages were displayed and sold where the public could not help but look on, the temptation to overindulge would be dominant. Following 1825, therefore, total abstinence societies sprang up. Members of these groups were subjected to severe persecution. Liquor makers and sellers hated them, for every convert they made meant the total loss of a customer. The abstainers' groups were not to be cowed or turned back, however, and the increase in the number of abstainers continued. By 1829, at least four hundred merchants in New England had closed out their bars. Total pledges for abstinence had gone beyond the one hundred thousand mark and continued to grow.

Concrete steps toward an organized fight for nationwide abstinence got under way. In 1829, the friends of sobriety held a general meeting at which the New York Temperance Society was organized. This movement came as a result of the untiring efforts of a retired businessman, Edward C. Delavan. President Jeremiah Day of Yale University became head of the Connecticut Temperance Society. The Hon. Lewis Case, of Michigan, twice in the United States cabinet, began a personal crusade for sobriety. In 1831, he was secretary of war and excluded the sale of alcoholic beverages from all army camps and to enlisted men. Abstinence continued to spread until nearly half the distilleries in New York had closed, and a survey showed that "prohibition has saved the state no less than six and one half million dollars in one year."

By 1833, there were no less than 5,000 temperance groups in the nation with 1,250,000 members of whom 12,000 were former drunkards who had become ardent crusaders for the abolition of the liquor traffic. Four thousand distilleries had closed down (in those days any individual or small mill could operate a distillery); 6,000 merchants had closed their bars; 4,000 ships of various tonnages had forbidden alcoholic beverages on board. That year the National Temperance Convention was held in Philadelphia with 440 delegates from 19 states in attendance. It was a significant meeting. It called for the abolition of the traffic in alcoholic beverages; it reiterated its appeal for total abstinence instead of mere temperance. "Temperance which does not mean total abstinence is powerless to do permanent good," it declared. This was the real beginning of the national prohibition movement.

2. A Mighty Warrior Appears

On October 12, 1775, there was born in a New England home a lad, Lyman Beecher, who was destined to become one of the mighty voices in the struggle against legalized liquors. He was educated at Yale University and called to his ministry in 1810 as pastor of the Congregational Church in Litchfield, Connecticut. In his autobiography, he tells of the elaborate preparations that had been made for his ordination and induction into his pastorate. All the male members of the council drank, he reports. Liquors were paid for out of church funds, and before the examination had been finished many of the members of the group were "hilarious because of drink." Such a display in the name of the Christian religion shocked the sensitive soul of the young man. He attended two other ordinations and witnessed the same shameful behavior. Then he revolted against the corruption of the Christian religion of his day. "I took an oath before God that I would never attend another occasion of that kind," he reports. Dr. Beecher was soon a leading figure in the prohibition movement of the nation.

III. The Noble Experiment

Every student of the history of prohibition is familiar with the contention of the liquor forces that the Eighteenth Amendment "was put over on the American people as a result of war hysteria." How far from the truth this statement is may readily be seen by looking at a few of the numerous authoritative books on this subject.

1. *During Revolutionary Days*

Friends of sobriety were distressed by the intemperate use of alcoholic beverages during colonial days. When the Revolutionary War broke loose they began to take drastic steps to curb their use throughout the colonies. In 1774, Anthony Benezet published a tract exposing the evil effects of alcohol. Three years later, Benjamin Rush,

M.D., a signer of the Declaration of Independence, published a pamphlet setting forth the harmful effects of alcoholic beverages. This was printed by the War Board of the Continental Congress and distributed among the soldiers. However, Dr. Rush's exposé was aimed primarily against distilled spirits. On March 25, 1776, General Washington issued a general order to all officers to do all they could to restrain the use of beverages by the soldiers. September 20, 1776, the Continental Congress prohibited the sale of distilled spirits to enlisted men.

In 1790, the College of Physicians and Surgeons of New York presented to the United States Senate a memorial against the use of spirits and urged that high duties be placed upon all imported beverages. Prohibition was on its way. But the liquor industry found a friend in Alexander Hamilton who, in 1791, succeeded in pushing temperance movements aside in favor of a revenue bill which put heavier taxes and licenses upon the manufacture and sale of all alcoholic beverages. He enlisted the Congress by his estimate of $800,000 per year from such taxes. What he did not foresee was the Whiskey Rebellion which cost the young nation $1,500,000. And legislators are still beguiled by the false claim that taxes on such beverages increase national net income!

2. Rising Religious Opposition

Prior to 1814, the year the second war with England closed, the religious bodies, with the exception of the Quakers, had done little against the liquor industry. In fact, religious festivities of almost every kind included drinking. But the devastation which always follows the use of alcohol as a beverage aroused bitter opposition. The writings of Increase Mather, Francis McKenzie,

Cotton Mather, John Wesley, and others had been widely circulated and bore their fruits. In 1814, the United Brethren incorporated in their discipline a rule limiting the use of alcohol to medicinal purposes. In 1821, they debarred distillers from church membership and urged all ministers to labor against the evils of intemperance. In 1826, the Congregationalists, led by Lyman Beecher, moved against the use of alcohol as a beverage. By 1820, the good effects of withholding liquors from enlisted men were so evident that Commissary General George Gibson, acting with the approval of Secretary of War Calhoun, issued an order that gave all soldiers cash value instead of the liquor ration. In 1833, the Baptists of Boston, Massachusetts, reported no members engaged in the liquor traffic.

3. Pre-Civil War Days

In 1827, Virginia joined the states having organized antiliquor societies. Social welfare groups had been investigating the relation between poverty and crime and the use of alcohol. In 1827, trustees of an almshouse in Baltimore, Maryland, checked the 623 inmates and found that 554 of them were paupers because of the effects of alcoholic beverages. The following year the Connecticut Medical Society came out in favor of control and the General Conference of the Methodist Church approved total abstinence. In 1830, a W.C.T.U. was organized in Ohio and the Chickasaw Indian tribe adopted the first prohibition law. There were that year more than one thousand temperance societies in the nation.

Then came startling discoveries by Dr. James Kirk, of Scotland. By checking the brains of victims of drink, he always found alcohol. In the brain tissue of an alcoholic

woman who had just died he found enough to see it burn
in a teaspoon into which he had drained some of the
brain content. Prohibition forces soon had strong back-
ing from the medical world. Conditions became so bad
in the nation's capital that the board of health banned all
sales for ninety days because they had become a public
nuisance. Secretary of War Lewis Case banned all liquor
sales in forts, camps, and such. In 1833, Georgia recognized the right of her citizens to local option control of
the traffic, Liberty and Camden Counties having peti-
tioned for that right.

4. Reaching the Climax

Following the days of reconstruction, the movement
against beverage alcohol began to take on new strength
and to spread rapidly throughout the nation. Much information had been accumulated by medical societies con-
demning alcohol as an arch traitor to human health and
well-being. In 1874, the National W.C.T.U. was organized. In 1884, the National Prohibition Party was set up.
The prohibition movement was handicapped for many
years by the lack of an integrating, directive agency. But
the Anti-Saloon League was set up June 4, 1893, in Ober-
lin, Ohio. Two years later the national league was organized in Washington City. From then on temperance
forces had a unified impact upon American politics.

At a national meeting of dry forces in Columbus, Ohio,
in 1913, the demand for a constitutional prohibition
amendment was crystallized. Former Governor Malcolm
Patterson of Tennessee, Ernest H. Cherrington of the
Temperance Publishing House, and Mrs. Lillian M.
Stevens of the W.C.T.U. were authorized to present the
matter to Congress. Congressman Richmond Pearson

Hobson, hero of the Spanish-American War, was chosen as their spokesman. But the resolution which he introduced failed to receive the two-thirds vote required for passage. In 1915, Senator Morris Sheppard of Texas introduced another such resolution. It was favorably reported by the House Judiciary Committee in 1916 but it was not until December 18, 1917, that the measure was adopted and the amendment submitted to the states. By 1919 it had been ratified by 46 of the states. The Eighteenth Amendment became effective January 16, 1920.

Thus it can be seen that the struggle against the traffic in beverage alcohol is not a new one and that the claim that national prohibition was a result of war hysteria is false. The beverage alcohol business had its way over a long period of time, during which many efforts were made by various people and organizations for its control. But always it broke down restraints, and the populace suffered from its disregard of human rights. As long as human nature is unchanged and men are allowed to seek wealth by whatever means they may find it, the traffic in narcotics and opiates will go on, and alcohol is a narcotic drug. So the movement toward complete destruction of legalized manufacture and sale of beverage alcohol must continue, will continue, and some day the useless, parasitical liquor industry will be removed from the national economy.

SUGGESTED TOPICS FOR DISCUSSION

1. Make a list of business enterprises that are antisocial in nature and tell how they should be handled by the government.
2. Make a list of the various temperance movements with which members of the class have been affiliated.
3. What causes temperance movements to wane in power and to lose grounds they have gained during periods of great effort?

CHAPTER 8 *OUTLINE*

I. CLEAN THE LAMP

   1. Sifting Propaganda
   2. Beware of Advertising
   3. How It Works
   4. Avoid Extremes
   5. Why Do They Drink?

II. HUMAN RIGHTS MUST PREVAIL

   1. Social Strength Sapped
   2. The Home Broken
   3. Political Units Impaired
   4. Care for Dependents Increased

III. SOCIAL CONTROL IMPERATIVE

   1. Licensing Opens Doors
   2. Rigid Restraints Demanded

IV. THE CALL TO CHURCHES

   1. Hold High Standards for Members
   2. Enlarge Scope of Education
   3. Befriend the Weak
   4. Provide Suitable Recreation
   5. Promote Righteousness

8

LET US REASON TOGETHER

ACROSS THE AGES wise men have noticed the debasing effects of alcohol upon people and have sought by counsel as well as by ridicule to bring people to realize that only the foolish will allow themselves to become victims of a thirst which, once formed, grips the soul like chains of steel, seldom to be broken without the aid of persistent friends or of divine power. Sober reasoning should mark all who are being tempted to imbibe alcoholic beverages or who wish to be prepared to engage in the warfare forever needed to help free mankind from people who for the sake of easy money make the narcotic drug available to unwary souls.

I. CLEAN THE LAMP

Many people yet live who know what it means to clean the chimney of an old-fashioned kerosene lamp. Unless watched carefully, the wick which conveyed the oil from the bowl to the burner would be befouled, the flame would grow uneven, and the glass chimney would be smoked. Unless often cleaned and polished the light from the lamp would become dim and flickering. Nowhere is there greater need for clear light than in the study of alcohol and its relations to human degeneracy and ruin.

1. Sifting Propaganda

Any study of recent publications which deal with alcoholic beverages and human welfare will show how personal interests control most of the information which is sent out about them. One treatise on the subject, written by a physician, will make it appear that alcohol is an innocent victim of prejudices which reformers and ignorant scientists stir up among the peoples of the land. Careful reading will reveal that the author is a drinker. If it is a treatise on the sociological aspects of the subject it will expose the curse that lies in the bottle, regardless of who uses it. Those who are set to profit from the liquor business or whose families are engaged in it will point out every possible fallacious argument which their opponents make and seek to dress up drinking as a social grace which none need fear except those who are inherently weak of will and unstable in character. One should always check the background from which any article or book on the subject comes.

2. Beware of Advertising

Advertising media have no more astute customers than the makers and vendors of alcoholic beverages. These customers are not stingy in their contributions to the profits of such media. Tear from any widely-read magazine all the liquor advertisements and calculate the amount paid for them; one is surprised at how much the magazine realizes from such propaganda. Radio is also widely used, especially by the makers of beer and wine. The propaganda sent abroad through radio channels is not limited to paid commercials; the subtle part is that which appears in the stories, soap box operas, and other dramatized features. Television is coming more and more to play its part in the field of liquor propaganda for, while distilled spirits are not allowed commercial time, the screen carries a more effective form of propaganda, the drinking scenes where all the allurements of the bottle are presented and few of the evils that flow from its use are suggested. Children witness such scenes; liquor makers place at their disposal soft drinks in containers which are exact replicas of bottles and cans which carry the intoxicants to the public; thus little minds are bent toward drink before reason has come.

3. How It Works

One little word will often spell the difference between truth and dangerous falsehood, and liquor propaganda knows how and when to use it. For example, about 1946, an advertisement was widely used by a whiskey maker. It showed an attractive scene on the lawn of a golf club. Four players were seated about a table on which a bottle of the brand of whiskey made by this company was standing. Before each man stood a sparkling glass in which ice cooled the drink from the bottle. In the branch of a tree above them two robins were seated and the male was saying to the female, "So that's why they would play only nine holes." One letter made the difference between subtle propaganda and truth. That line should have read, "That's why they *could* play only nine holes." Everyone familiar with the effects of alcohol knows that two or three nips from that bottle readily made it impossible for the men to play a satisfactory game, more probably made them unwilling to leave the bottle in order to do anything else.

Friends of sobriety need always to be alert. Such propaganda should be studied. Exposure should be made of all such subtle and misleading publicity about alcoholic beverages as is flooding the land today through advertising media of every kind. At least once each month churches and schools should post on their bulletin boards samples of the advertising and point out how misleading and insidious it is. Public roadside billboards are being used effectively in some areas to counteract such advertising. Floats featuring wrecked cars, with dummies to represent dead motorists, make a tremendous impression wherever used in parades. Paid copy needs to be furnished to the press, especially to papers that refuse to carry liquor advertisements. Over radio and on TV screens, children and youths should be made aware of the subtle way by which the liquor interests cover up the sin and shame, the debauchery and crime, the mental and physical illness, and the premature death to which such drinking scenes often lead. Parents cannot make a servant drunk, as the ancient Spartan parents did, in order to show how silly it is to drink, but they can visit police courts and the jails and workhouses and see what drink does. Most police departments will provide a speaker for school or church or club, there to tell how drinking affects society, how it doubles the crime load which taxpayers carry, how it debases habitual users and robs society of their talents and productive toil.

4. *Avoid Extremes*

One does not need to spend time refuting the claims of the brewers that beer contains food. As shown in a previous chapter, the oxidation of the alcohol generates a bit of heat; the sugar content of the bottle of beer is a food element, and there remains a bit of the vegetable matter which fermentation did not destroy. Do not spend time in denying that there is a modicum of food in a glass of beer; show how the buyer of the brew has been duped by the brewers into paying a big price for a morsel of food, while at the same time paying for a narcotic drug which he has to drink in order to get the food. For the same money which is paid for a bottle of beer one can get far more vitamins and calories from other sources and not have to swallow a habit-forming drug in order to eat or drink.

One must be on guard against the emotional appeal in the claim, "The alcoholic is a sick man." Police registers still carry them as ordinary drunks. Let the makers and vendors of liquors find what consolation they can in removing the stigma of drunkenness from the victim of their product. In turn, cast scorching satire upon the claim. Keep continuously before the public the fact that the liquor industry caused the sickness. Magnify the folly of any society that would tolerate for a day an enemy alien who came to scatter disease-breeding germs among the unsuspecting citizens, while earning good profits by the sale of the stuff containing them. Then show that that would be similar to what the vendors of alcoholic beverages do when they dispense the potion which brings upon millions of victims the alcoholic sickness.

5. Why Do They Drink?

There is great need for light to be shed on the claim of the liquor forces regarding the cause of alcoholism. Three professors of Rutgers University made a careful and unbiased check of a large number of drinkers from various cultural groups. They discovered that 43 per cent of them drank for reasons of sociability. Knowing this fact enables one to understand why the liquor interests are so persistent in seeking to make the nation believe that social drinking is "the thing." The Yale School of Alcohol Studies reported: "Forty per cent of drinking is symptomatic of inner or environmental maladjustments, while 60 per cent is purely social." So the claim that people become alcoholics because of inferiority complexes or because of personality defects is disproved. Such defects may hasten them on to becoming alcoholics but they do not cause them to drink; alcohol in their drinks dethrones the will regardless of the person.

"Highly paid trade lobbyists in Hollywood effectively keep the drink habit before the public as well as keeping the bad effects of drink off the screen." [1] There is no relief from this subtle and dangerous propaganda unless the Federal government steps in to bar all liquor propaganda from the United States mails. Public safety, national security, public health, and the general welfare all clamor for this step in rigid social control to be taken before the growing generation has been led by propaganda into the coils of strong drink.

II. HUMAN RIGHTS MUST PREVAIL

Any sociologist of worth, any student of democratic processes in government, or anyone familiar with the teachings of the Bible knows well that the individual is the basic unit of any social group, whether family, precinct, county, state, or nation. It is, therefore, axiomatic that whatever affects the individual also affects the social group. If he is benefited by any occupation or trade and by any expenditure of his earnings, society is benefited. If

---

[1] Charles M. Crowe, "Repeal After Twenty Years," *The Christian Century*, Feb. 14, 1951, p. 206.

he is debased in spirit or handicapped in body, society to that extent is injured. Looking at the trade in alcoholic beverages with this truth in mind, what do we find?

1. *Social Strength Sapped*

"Whatever cripples the individual undermines the state" is more than a trite remark; it is an undeniable truth. Jesus set this sociological law as the bedrock of all human relationships when he classed the commandment "Thou shalt love thy neighbour as thyself" (Matt. 19:19) with the commandment to love God and serve only him. One is not, therefore, acting merely as a reformer when he challenges the right of any individual or group to sell a product which blasts character, weakens minds, breaks up homes, and produces crime and poverty. Every citizen is acting with prophetic foresight and patriotic devotion when he seeks to create a government that will refuse permission to every citizen to operate any business which earns its profits by debasing the citizenry whom the state rules and upon whom all social and political groups are dependent for security and well-being.

2. *The Home Broken*

Wherever there is an alcoholic, there is a disrupted family circle. How far strong drink has gone in creating concern for American homes was revealed through a check by the author of more than three hundred high school students. In response to the request for information about what they would like to find in a study like *Shadow Over America*, a large per cent of them replied, "How it affects the home." Quite evidently young people everywhere are familiar with the way alcohol is disrupting the American home. A study made in Philadelphia showed that between 1937 and 1950 one of every five divorces was directly due to alcohol. Since drunkenness is not a ground for divorce in the state, the actual part played by alcoholic beverages in breaking homes in that city is not revealed. Other surveys show that homes broken by drinking produce a far larger per cent of juvenile criminals than do homes where drinking is not allowed. Drinkers may, as one writer claims, produce more children than do sober people but they also provide the nation with more broken homes and an increased number of criminals.

3. *Political Units Impaired*

Crime runs rampant across any country that permits any segment of the populace to fatten its purse by the sale of alcoholic beverages. The F.B.I. report for 1955 showed crime up 26 per cent since 1950. Since a large proportion of arrests are in connection with drinking anyone can easily see what a price a political unit has to pay for tolerating legal sales. Whether town, city, county, state, or nation, wisdom would lead its citizenry to bar all outlets for so prolific a breeder of crime as is beverage alcohol.

4. *Care for Dependents Increased*

A grand jury in Los Angeles, California, closed its report in a recent year with these words: "Our jails and prisons are crowded; our courts and police organizations are burdened; our law enforcement and social welfare problems are seriously aggravated because of the licensed liquor traffic. . . . The tax costs now falling on the innocent citizenry because of the liquor traffic are intolerable." And yet there are church members who believe that liquor should be legalized because of the tax revenues it produces!

III. SOCIAL CONTROL IMPERATIVE

There is no known way to keep the traffic in any narcotic drug from falling into evil hands. In other words, the dope peddler and the bootlegger and moonshiner are inseparable from the product which each dispenses. The effort to control the traffic in alcoholic beverages by licensing some people to carry it on fails on several counts.

1. *Licensing Opens Doors*

Legalizing sales of alcoholic beverages opens the advertising media to the dealers as well as manufacturers, and they create by subtle publicity both a desire for their products and the idea that it is safe to use them. High pressure salesmen are thereby permitted to persuade even churchmen that the liquor industry is a reputable business, hence that anyone can with dignity engage in it. By allowing for the seductive display of wares and the continuous appeal to appetites, license assures the liquor industry of freedom to inflame the desire of all victims of drink and to add a steady increase to the number of its customers. But legalizing the sales does not lessen the evils which always come from alcoholic beverages; it only opens the way for a few citizens to earn big profits while adding to the burden of taxpayers who provide protection and customers for the liquor industry, confinement in prison for criminals whom it produces, and support for dependents whom its products inevitably create. An honest and accurate evaluation of the facts should cause every voter to realize that the alcohol problem will never be solved by putting the making and selling of beverages under the dignity of governmental sanction.

Instead of putting an end to illegal manufacture and the illicit sale of alcoholic beverages, license only provides a blind behind which the criminals may operate. Many years ago, when there were 550 licensed saloons in Louisville, Kentucky, a local newspaper reported bootlegging rampant. Moonshine stills are frequently captured today. Other criminals of the liquor traffic are notoriously prevalent in and around American cities where liquor stores, barrooms, taverns, and such are to be found on every hand.

2. *Rigid Restraints Demanded*

"You can't keep the rain from falling," said a Tennessee countryman when devastating floods were once coursing down the Tennessee River. "No," replied a United States engineer, "but we can build a system of dams along the river that will stop it from destroying life and property." And that is what has been done. Even so, a system of control can be worked out by the Federal government that will harness the alcohol industry and so govern it that damage from it in the future will be brought to a very insignificant minimum.

The first step in this direction must be the control of production. The manufacture of commercial alcohol should be placed in the hands of carefully chosen and supervised producers. Rigid rules should govern them to the end that their product cannot be converted into ethyl alcohol and that their sales are only to individuals and firms licensed to use such in their business.

The manufacture of ethyl alcohol should be carried on by only a few producers whose capacity would insure only the amount of this narcotic drug needed regularly for such uses as are approved by medical associations and by representative chemical concerns. All other equipment now used in the manufacture of alcoholic beverages should be paid for and, when not convertible to other uses, destroyed.

Control of distribution is equally important if beverage alcohol is to be removed from the commanding place it now occupies in the land. The distribution of all products containing ethyl alcohol should be placed under the restrictions that govern the sales of morphine, opium, and other such drugs. A careful check should be kept on physicians who write prescriptions calling for this product. Penalties for violation of the laws governing the distribution of ethyl alcohol should be as severe and as rigidly enforced as they are against the sale of opiates.

IV. The Call to Churches

Every harmful practice among men is a challenge to the forces set up to promote the physical and moral well-being of mankind. There should, therefore, be no compromise between Christians and the beverage alcohol industry. If the follower of Christ is to abstain from every form of evil (1 Thess. 5:22), he must abstain from the purchase and use of alcoholic beverages, since a whole multitude of evils grows out of both the sale and the use of such drinks. To be successful in averting the dangers which always threaten society where alcoholic beverages are available to people, the churches should plan and carry out a very comprehensive program.

1. Hold High Standards for Members

The story of the Good Samaritan should impel every Christian to be both a total abstainer from alcoholic beverages and a vigorous opponent of the entire liquor industry. How can one look upon the pitiable state of alcoholics and continue to argue that men have a right to sell the drink that causes their condition? It is like asserting that a man has a right to let a vicious dog run loose, regardless of how many people it bites. To give consent to the traffic in alcoholic beverages because one is an abstainer and is not hurt by the traffic is like asserting lack of responsibility for letting a blind man run into a pit which careless man has left uncovered.

The Bible specifically condemns one who gives drink to his neighbor (Hab. 2:15). Is one who sells the drink to the neighbor less of a sinner? Every minister is commanded to be an example to them that believe, in word and in manner of life (1 Tim. 4:12). Can the minister who drinks beer or wine or cocktails be the right example to youths or to adults who watch him? Peter's admonition to the elders or pastors against "lording it over the charge allotted to you" (1 Pet. 5:3 ASV), should make all ministers know that they have no right to drink wine or beer. The Christlike example is given by Paul and should govern all believers. It is, "It is good not to eat flesh, nor to drink wine, nor to do anything whereby thy brother stumbleth" (Rom. 14:21 ASV). Churches will not possess the power Christ would have them use unless they demand that their members keep this rule of conduct in mind.

2. *Enlarge Scope of Education*

The statement of the Master, "Ye shall know the truth, and the truth shall make you free" (John 8:32) is as true today as it was when he uttered it. Facts are needed, not fancies, when one goes before the court of public opinion. So there is great need for an increased emphasis upon what once was called temperance education. Churches must lead out in this work. To the end that suitable materials may be available for all age groups, the graded series of studies, of which *Shadow Over America* is a part, has been prepared. Teaching about the dangers inherent in the use of beverage alcohol should begin in the home. Thoroughgoing information about it as well as about other narcotics should be given from early childhood, and churches have a good opportunity of supplementing home training through the Sunday schools. The press should be used freely in exposing the fallacious and seductive advertising of the liquor industry. The quarterly temperance lessons in Sunday school should be emphasized and often supplemented by special features such as dramatized stories, personal testimonies about the value of abstinence, human interest stories about victims of strong drink, through special speakers and public forums. Citizens everywhere should see to it that unimpeded instruction about alcohol be given in the public schools. Materials for all such instruction may be had from various religious publishing houses, from the temperance organizations, and by watching the reports of all law-enforcing agencies of the land.

3. *Befriend the Weak*

While doing all in their power to prevent the people from taking the first drink, the churches must not forget their obligation to the victims of alcohol. Imbibing this narcotic is dangerous to all, regardless of the trade name under which it is sold. For one of every nine who indulges in its use it is dangerous, since it makes him an alcoholic. With the number of drinkers increasing and the problems that grow out of drink multiplying, the churches have a serious task before them in providing some shelter for victims of the craving for strong drink.

There is need, therefore, in every congregation for a capable committee to plan strategies against the liquor industry and to rescue victims of alcohol who live on the church field. While doing everything possible to save young people from taking the first drink, such a committee should work to keep moderate drinkers from continuing to jeopardize their future, and to liberate alcoholics from slavery.

In the effort to rescue victims of the lust for strong drink, especially the alcoholics, one must bring them to take three important steps. The drinker must be led to desire freedom, hence should be led to overcome his self-pity and to master the defeatest spirit within him. He then must be led to hate the thing that enslaves him and the industry that produces it and goes to such extremes to induce people—all people—to use it. While he must not be taught to hate people, he can be led to have a righteous hatred for the industry and will thereby be led to desire to cease patronizing it. Finally, he must be led to pray earnestly and often for deliverance from the curse. By being led with tact and patience, guided by genuine love, many a victim of alcohol can be set free from the alcohol habit.

4. *Provide Suitable Recreation*

Since it is a fact that more than half of all users of alcoholic beverages begin as social drinkers, it is quite evident that to provide needed social activities for people will remove the strongest incentive they have for drink. Man is a gregarious creature; he must have outlets for his instinctive desire for fellowship with other people. Let these be provided by the forces of sobriety, and the places that serve liquors will immediately begin to lose customers. As long as friends of sobriety spend time railing about the bright lights and luxurious furnishings of liquor stores and the subtle entertainment provided in taverns, cabarets, roadhouses, and clubs, they will make no headway in their fight against alcohol. It is up to parents, schools, civic groups, and churches to enter upon a long-range program of providing recreational facilities for as many as they can possibly serve. They who plan cities or new subdivisions for the future should be wise enough to see that adequate lands for public playgrounds shall be set aside. The more of natural exercise and wholesome fun any people get, the less desire they will have for the sordid amusements associated with drinking.

The great majority of people know little about how to play. With limited facilities for recreation, it becomes ever more necessary that schedules for various age groups be set up. In this way intensive activities can be provided so as to burn up in the limited time the maximum amount of energy which, when not burned through wholesome exercise, leads to harmful outlets, usually connected with the use of liquors. A well-planned and directed program of community activities will always go far toward solving the crime problem. Instead of leaving people to turn to drink, they can be given fellowship and fun where drink is never seen and thus kept from temptation.

5. *Promote Righteousness*

"Righteousness exalteth a nation" (Prov. 14:34), so let no one be ashamed of putting forth every possible effort to cause people to desire to be good, law-abiding, sober, diligent, industrious citizens. Keep continuously before the people of all ages the beauty of holiness. How much more honorable it is to keep the lips from profanity than it is to pour forth vulgar and profane words. Show by precept as well as by example the difference between the alcoholic and the sober person, between the tipsy host or guest and the person whose culture is so fine he does not need to stoop to the artificial freedom which drink may give. Make very clear that the finest athletes, the greatest soldiers, the most trustworthy pilots on land or sea or in the air, and most of the world's great geniuses have been abstainers. Develop the spirit of patriotism that makes one willing to forego personal pleasures for the sake of the larger good, and fan the flames of individual ambition to where the desire for freedom which total abstinence provides will act as a giant bulwark against the propaganda of the liquor forces and thus make America not only a safe champion of democracy but able to safeguard the democracy that she champions.

Abraham Lincoln was riding one day with a wealthy friend. As they journeyed, the gentleman offered Mr. Lincoln a cigar of a very rare kind. Mr. Lincoln declined in his awkward but gracious manner. A bit further on the man offered Mr. Lincoln a drink of some very choice whiskey, and again the President declined. Finally the gentleman rather urged the President to drink, whereupon Mr. Lincoln replied: "My mother died when I was nine years of age. Before she went away she had me promise that I would never use tobacco or drink intoxicants. I have kept that promise until this day. Perhaps I should now break it and drink with you. What do you say?" The man thought for a moment then turned to Mr.

Lincoln and said: "I would be far better off if my mother had exacted a promise of the kind from me. No, sir, you ought not to break it." And because he did not break it he has influenced hosts of others to refrain from the cup that condemns so many millions to bondage in the flesh and to premature death.

Before the manuscript of this book was completed, *The Cup of Fury,* by Upton Sinclair, came from the press. In it the noted author, who has been called the Charles Dickens of America, presents word pictures of a number of famous writers whose lives were wrecked by alcoholic beverages and who went to premature graves, several as suicides. He tells the story of social drinking which led to alcoholism and premature death to Jack London, O. Henry, Sinclair Lewis, Edna St. Vincent Millay, and many others. It is a gripping exposé of drinking and the liquor traffic. When this book had been read there came with fresh appeal the tragic question of Bill Day, uttered decades ago in a railway commissary car, "Why do men do it, Clerk? Why?"

SUGGESTED TOPICS FOR DISCUSSION

1. Make a list of all the organizations in your community that are working to impart information about alcohol.
2. What program of recreation could your church set up with its present facilities? With some added equipment?
3. Make a list of ways in which Christian citizens may help make America a sober nation.
4. Read carefully *Education for Sobriety* by Helen McKnight and make suggestions about a program of alcohol education for your church.

QUESTIONS FOR REVIEW AND EXAMINATION

CONCERNING the examination and the requesting of awards, see Directions for the Teaching and the Study of This Book for Credit, page 135.

CHAPTER 1

1. How can the use of wine through the years be explained?
2. Tell how fermentation takes place.
3. Why should alcohol and other narcotic drugs be controlled?
4. What does society pay for legalizing intoxicants?

CHAPTER 2

5. What lessons may be learned from ancient Grecian kings?
6. What did Moses have to say about strong drink?
7. What advice did Lemuel's mother give him about drink?
8. Tell of some Hebrews who refused to drink.
9. Why did Paul advise Timothy to drink wine?
10. How does drinking cast shadows over America?

CHAPTER 3

11. What does alcohol do to the body's control system?
12. Name some ways in which alcohol brings danger and harm.
13. How does alcohol undermine one's health?
14. How does alcohol harm the heart?

CHAPTER 4

15. Why is the claim that one must be either an alcoholic or something worse a false one?
16. What are the dangers of drinking?
17. Show how control of the production and sale of alcohol tends to lessen its use.
18. How does the liquor industry seek to get people to drink its products?
19. Who should worry about drinking?
20. Name four ways in which alcohol harms the individual and society.

CHAPTER 5

21. What three factors are necessary to the well-being of a free people?
22. Why is alcohol the enemy of a democratic nation?
23. How does alcohol affect the offspring of alcoholics?
24. Give illustrations of how the use of alcohol causes innocent people to suffer.
25. Why is drinking so dangerous where modern machines are operated?

CHAPTER 6

26. What is man's fourfold task on earth?
27. Show how the use of alcoholic beverages interferes with man's task.
28. Why are sober citizens needed?
29. Give reasons for national control of all outlets for beverage alcohol.
30. What does the Bible teach about alcohol as a food?
31. Tell how the Bible condemns wine as a beverage.
32. What admonition does the Bible give to the victim of strong drink?

CHAPTER 7

33. Why is liquor used so much in southern Europe?
34. How has Britain been harmed by drinking?
35. What caused opposition to the liquor industry to arise in Great Britain?
36. Give some of the steps taken during colonial days to curb the use of alcohol.
37. How did national prohibition come about?

CHAPTER 8

38. Why should one use care in accepting information about the liquor traffic?
39. Why is liquor advertising so deceptive?
40. Why do people drink alcoholic beverages?
41. How does alcohol damage the individual?
42. What does drinking do to the home?
43. Why should every Christian be a total abstainer?

SUGGESTIONS TO THE TEACHER

THE TEACHER who would render the most effective service for the cause of sobriety must be thoroughly convinced that the lessons to be taught are of vital importance. He will need to keep in mind that there may be some in the class who drink occasionally. Some may have alcoholics in their families. Some may have been beguiled by liquor propaganda. It is likely that few of the class members understand the significance and the scope of the liquor problem today.

If at all possible, master the subject, chapter by chapter, before each class period. Make use of books such as those listed in the Bibliography if they are available.

When possible, secure living witnesses—people who were once heavy drinkers but who have now been rehabilitated. Special emphasis can be brought by presenting one or more of the sketches from Upton Sinclair's *The Cup of Fury*.

On the first four evenings, assign to one or more members of the class one of the "Suggested Topics for Discussion" and call for a report the next night.

Illustrations help people to remember. Seek them from every possible source. The newspapers often provide abundant illustrative material. The illustrations given by the author will serve as examples. But the best examples will be those provided by the teacher from his own observation and experience and by class members.

Seek to enlist the class in some positive program of action for sobriety as a result of this study.

BIBLIOGRAPHY

BOOKS

ORDER any books listed from your denominational book store.

The Christian Case for Abstinence. New York: Association Press, 1955. $3.00.

Earle, Clifford. *Alcohol and Christian Responsibility.* Philadelphia: Board of Christian Education, Presbyterian Church in the U.S.A. 65¢.

Emerson, Haven, M.D. *Alcohol, Its Effects on Man.* New York: Appleton-Century-Crofts, 1936. $1.00.

Fox, Ruth, M.D., and Lyon, Peter. *Alcoholism: Its Scope, Cause and Treatment.* New York: Random House, 1955. $3.00.

Harmsworth, Harry C. *A Survey of the Alcohol and Narcotics Problem in Idaho.* Moscow, Idaho: University of Idaho, 1954.

Hearn, C. Aubrey. *The Way to Sobriety.* Cincinnati: The Standard Publishing Foundation, 1955. $1.50.

King, Albion Roy. *Basic Information on Alcohol.* Mount Vernon, Iowa: Cornell College Press, 1953.

Patrick, Clarence H. *Alcohol, Culture, and Society.* Durham: Duke University Press, 1952. $3.00.

Rea, Frederick B. *Alcoholism, Its Psychology and Cure.* London: The Epworth Press, 1956.

Sinclair, Upton. *The Cup of Fury.* Great Neck, New York: Channel Press, Inc., 1956. $3.00.

Straus, Robert, and Bacon, Selden D. *Drinking in College.* New Haven: Yale University Press, 1953. $4.00.

BOOKLETS

Hammaker, William E. *Drinking—Right or Wrong?* Columbus, Ohio: School & College Service, 1949. 50¢.

Hearn, C. Aubrey. *What About Drinking?* Columbus, Ohio: School and College Service, 1955. 30¢.

McKnight, Helen. *Education for Sobriety.* Pittsburgh, Pennsylvania: Temperance Education, 1954. 50¢.

Seliger, Robert V., M.D. *It's Smarter Not to Drink.* Columbus, Ohio: School & College Service, 1949. 25¢.

Order catalogues of booklets from the Methodist Board of Temperance, 100 Maryland Avenue, N. E., Washington, D.C., and the Signal Press, Evanston, Illinois.

ACKNOWLEDGMENTS

GRATEFUL ACKNOWLEDGMENT is made to the following publishers and authors for kind permission to use the copyrighted selections in this volume:

Appleton-Century-Crofts, New York, for material from *Alcohol: Its Effects on Man,* by Haven Emerson.

The Christian Century for a quotation from an article.

Pageant Magazine for a brief quotation from an article.

School and College Service, Columbus, Ohio, for a quotation from *It's Smarter Not to Drink,* by Robert V. Seliger.

The Wheeler Publishing Company, Chicago, for several quotations from *Effects,* by Thurman B. Rice and Rolla N. Harger.

DIRECTIONS FOR THE TEACHING AND THE STUDY OF THIS BOOK FOR CREDIT

I. DIRECTIONS FOR THE TEACHER

1. Ten class periods of forty-five minutes each, or the equivalent, are required for the completion of this book for credit.

2. The teacher of the class will be given an award on the book if he requests it.

3. The teacher shall give a written examination covering the subject matter in the textbook, with at least one question or written assignment on each chapter, and the student shall make a minimum grade of 70 per cent. The written examination may take the form of assigned work to be done and written up between the class sessions, in the class sessions, or as a final written examination at the end of the course.

EXCEPTION: All who attend all of the class sessions; who read the book through by the close of the course; and who, in the judgment of the teacher, do the classwork satisfactorily may be exempted from taking the examination.

4. In the Graded Training Union Study Course, a seal for subject 3, The Christian Life, is granted to young people or adults for the completion of this book.

Sunday school credit may be elected by the pupil. Application for Sunday school awards should be sent to the state Sunday school department and for Training Union awards to the state Training Union department. These departments will provide the forms for these applications. They should be made in duplicate and both copies sent.

II. DIRECTIONS FOR THE STUDENT

1. *In Classwork*

(1) The pupil must attend at least six of the ten forty-five minute periods to be eligible to take the class examination.

(2) The pupil must certify that the textbook has been read. (In rare cases where pupils may find it impracticable to read the book before the completion of the classwork, the

teacher may accept a promise to read the book carefully within the next two weeks.)

(3) The pupil must take a written examination, with at least one question or written assignment from each chapter, making a minimum grade of 70 per cent. (All who attend all of the class sessions; who read the book through by the close of the course; and who, in the judgment of the teacher, do satisfactory classwork may be exempted from taking the examination.)

2. *In Individual Study by Correspondence*

Those who for any reason wish to study the book without the guidance of a teacher will use one of the following methods:

(1) Write answers to the questions printed in the book, or

(2) Write a summary of each chapter or a development of the chapter outlines.

If the second method is used, the student will study the book and then with the open book write the chapter summaries or a development of the chapter outlines.

In either case the student must read the book through.

Students may find profit in studying the text together, but where awards are requested, individual papers are required. Carbon copies or duplicates in any form cannot be accepted.

All written work done by such students on books for Sunday school credit should be sent to the state Sunday school secretary. All of such work done on books for Training Union credit should be sent to the state Training Union secretary.

III. INTERCHANGE OF CREDITS AND AWARDS ON COMPARABLE SUBJECTS

One award, either for Training Union or Sunday school, is granted for completing this book.

J. E. LAMBDIN
Secretary, Training Union Department,
Baptist Sunday School Board

C. AUBREY HEARN
Director of the Study Course